# My Father Will Kill Me
# My Mother Will Die

Seeds of Shame – Harvest of Hope

Published by Lifespan Coaching & Consulting, L.L.C.
415 N. Academy Drive
Ephrata, PA 17522
https://www.lifespan.center

Print ISBN: 978-1-7372349-0-6
eBook ISBN: 978-1-7372349-1-3

# My Father Will Kill Me
# My Mother Will Die

## Seeds of Shame – Harvest of Hope

Joan E. Boydell

# What Others Are Saying

"This book has a shocking title—a cry of despair and hopelessness that rings familiar to anyone in the helping professions. But in these remarkable pages, Joan Boydell brings to life story after story of healing, hope, and redemption, as she recounts the challenges in her own life and a lifetime of helping others turn those cries of anguish into songs of joy. Readers can learn much from Joan's skill in compassionately listening to those who are in fear and offer them the remedy of Perfect Love—that love that comes from God."

—**MICHAEL GEER**, President, PA Family Institute

"It has been said that stories are one of the most powerful ways to influence and inspire people. In *My Father Will Kill Me, My Mother Will Die*, Joan Boydell masterfully shares her life through compelling stories about the people she has touched along the way and how they have touched her. Her storytelling cadence is rhythmic and refreshing and inspires readers to consider as divine the encounters God puts in their paths.

Those whose daily lives are immersed in the complexities of others' lives will especially enjoy Joan's perspective and be encouraged to embrace vulnerability, honesty, and humility as they serve God by serving others."

—**CINDY HOPKINS**, CYNTHIA C. HOPKINS, MA,
Organizational Leadership Care Net Vice President
of Center Services & Client Care

"I am honored to have worked with Joan on this incredible collection of stories and insights. *My Father Will Kill Me, My Mother Will Die* is a thoughtful, poignant look into the lives of those who have made difficult decisions around unplanned pregnancies from a compassionate spiritual viewpoint. Her writing challenges us to see beyond the statistics and political posturing to see the hurting people behind them—people who desperately need to know and feel the love of their Creator through the sacrificial love of his people. I believe God will use this book in a mighty way to encourage those in service of others to see a higher perspective in their work to not grow weary in doing well."

—**BETH LOTTIG**, Editor, Founder of Inspire Books

"Powerful, unique, and overdue are the three words that best describe *My Father Will Kill Me, My Mother Will Die: Seeds of Shame—Harvest of Hope*. Using a novel combination of Scripture, quotes, music, poems, and her own life experiences,

Joan Boydell ingeniously connects true stories of people facing life's most traumatic circumstances to provide education and advice on how to best help people. The book may move you to tears or bring you joy. Prayerfully, it will equip, motivate, and inspire you to continue the mission we are all called to—to reach others with the love of our Savior, Jesus Christ."

—**JEANNEANE MAXON, J.D.**,
Nationally Recognized Speaker and Human Rights Advocate
Five-year Terminal Cancer Survivor, Former General Counsel of Care Net
Former Vice President of External Affairs of Americans United for Life

"I was deeply honored when I was asked to write an endorsement for Joan's book, which I had been encouraging her to write for many years. I had the privilege of serving under her wise tutelage as client services director during her tenure as executive director at the pregnancy center. I know you will be blessed and inspired as you read about Joan's personal story interwoven with her experience. You will sense her deeply compassionate heart as she shares the ups and downs of ministering alongside women and men facing the crisis of unplanned pregnancy. Be prepared to experience the full gamut of emotions as you take this journey. Her book will touch and encourage you."

—**JANE "GOLDIE" WINN, MSS**, Certified Life Coach
Client Advocate at Palm Beach Women's Clinic, Boca Raton, FL
Author of *Rainbow in the Night: A Journey of Redemption*

"For those who serve as volunteers, staff, and board members with pregnancy resource centers, Joan extracts axioms for living from a broad spectrum of vignettes of people in crisis. She courageously engages the stories of clients as on-ramps to the highway of her own life story. Beneficially, these life experiences are grounded in references to the larger context of wisdom from the arts, professionals, and Scripture."

—**KEITH E. YODER, EdD**, Author and founder of
Teaching the Word Ministries

# DEDICATION

This book might not ever have been written without the encouragement and support of my husband, Bruce. He inspired me, helped me draw up an outline and plan, provided technical and formatting assistance, and took over some routine tasks to free up more of my time. When I became discouraged, he lifted my spirits. When I became too intense, he helped me laugh and relax. I finished the first full draft on February 14, 2021, almost exactly fifty-five and a half years after we were married. On that Valentine's Day, I pulled out a card he had written to me on February 14, 1981. It reads:

*Dear Joan,*

*Let no day go by without my expressing to you in some word or action my love for you and the deep place of gratitude I hold in my heart for your life being joined with mine and ours with Christ. I am reminded on this day of the joy I experience for what we have in common and for the unique person you are in God's plan and purpose.*

*Love, Bruce*

It is still true today!

The dedication of this book extends to my children, their spouses, and my grandchildren. They have contributed to the richness and fruitfulness of my life and are part of the ground from which the stories of this book have sprouted.

I am abundantly blessed!

# Table of Contents

# Foreword

I am so pleased that Joan has finally written this book that has been in her for years. It is a counselor's manual in narrative form. Joan is a seasoned veteran in the field, and I have witnessed her personal integrity, love for the Lord, love for people, and passion for healing. She covers hard-to-talk-about issues surrounding abortion, like physical and sexual trauma, self-mutilation, bulimia, borderline personality disorder, and sex trafficking. She describes the requisite attitudes and skills in helping people to navigate through these issues and even addresses self-care. She tackles the tough challenges of our current culture in a way that promotes honest dialogue. She speaks truth with a biblical foundation and authority. As a helping professional myself, these stories are encouraging me to be faithful to plant the seed from the One who gives the seed, even if I don't see the results. Her honesty and transparency are qualities shaped by the pain and struggles she experienced in earlier years that God is using to make her a powerful human paraclete and intercessor.

Your reading of this book will not only strengthen and

encourage you personally and professionally; it will also make you feel like you have had a personal encounter with a woman who speaks truth in love and is your friend.

VINCENT CALLOWAY
Master of Social Science
Licensed Clinical Social Worker
Certified Employee Assistance Professional
Currently in private practice, working with
children, adolescents, and adults

# Introduction

A story stays with you for a long time. After a three-part lecture is forgotten and the list of principles and practical applications have faded, an interesting story is still planted in your mind. Not every story needs to be told, but stories help to inform who we become and what we do. The master of parables has taught me that. I have been collecting stories in my mind and on paper for many years.

All the stories in this book are about real people and their real-life situations. The names have been changed and many details rearranged to protect their privacy. In many cases, the subjects in the stories have given permission for their stories to be told and have actually helped to write them. Some combine elements from several stories, stitched together for a purpose, that point in the same direction. Some stories I hold in my heart and will never be able to tell because they are too revealing. They span many years and occurred in a variety of settings. Many come from my time working in a pregnancy center or with others who work in pregnancy centers.

Pregnancy centers were started to help women and men

facing the issues of unplanned pregnancy. The stories in this book will help you understand some of the things they face, regardless of your opinions regarding abortion and pregnancy decisions. The center where I worked as executive director for almost twenty years served women and men from the diverse ethnic groups who populated our urban and suburban region. We had a team of young adults on our staff who spoke regularly in area middle schools and high schools and had a heavy schedule in the large nearby city. They related well! Although staff rotated over the years, for a few years we called it the "Dream Team" composed of a white woman, a black woman, an Asian man, and a Latino! A young black man with a powerful story later enhanced our team with his repertoire of original rap music!

The stories that form the content of this book are partly the offspring of my own personal story. Some stories go back further to my own school days, years teaching school and raising a family, living and working in a community group home setting, and counseling in private practice. Although most of them are more than two decades old, I am telling them now because they still have relatable value and may provide hope and inspiration to those who help others and those who are reaching out for hope. Like fine wine, the value of history is only appreciated after a season of fermentation. This book is timely.

Many things have changed over the last thirty years. More comprehensive laws are in place regarding child abuse, foster care, and adoption. Counseling agencies and pregnancy centers have much more well-developed guidelines and best practices. Ultrasound services did not become routine in obstetrical care until near the end of the twentieth century, so the use in pregnancy centers was not well established yet. Few were providing STD/STI testing. The important thing, however, is that the emotional impact of life-challenging events has not changed. Our understanding has grown tremendously as we see the magnitude of the powerful consequences of adverse events, especially in the early years of life.

There is one story that winds through all the others that is true in detail. It is as true as I can remember because it is my story of how God helped me to grow and get involved in the lives of others, starting before my college years, serving as a resident assistant and then assistant housemother in my college dorm. Most of my life, I have been drawn to other people who need someone to be with them, near them, in all kinds of circumstances. The song, "People", that Barbra Streisand made popular in the 1960s, still comes to mind.

I think of my father. He was the neighborhood fixit man, repairing broken machines and helping neighbors build or move things. He also was the first one on the scene to tend to a wounded or hurting child. I suppose I was the first one to cry when someone was hurt, as well as the first one to tremble in fear when there was anger and rebuke displayed. I needed other people, too.

Years ago, my husband, Bruce, and I sat at dinner with my

parents in their home. We were curious about some things from the past, and the mood was right for asking questions. Bruce asked them, "What was Joan like as a child?" My mother told this tale that I had never heard before. One day she took my brother and me and two other neighborhood children to the movies for a Disney show. I was not the youngest child, but something frightened and upset me, and I was inconsolable. Mom had to take me out of the theater and call our neighbor to pick me up because she could not calm me down. I was truly terrified. No one could remember what the movie even was. She concluded, though, by saying that I was often fearful. "Yes," my father said. "She was often afraid of new things." As I reread this notation recently, I had an aha moment. I had seen a quick picture somewhere of a scene from the original Dumbo movie, where older nasty elephants stood mocking the tenderhearted little Dumbo with the big floppy ears. The timing would have been right for a reshowing of that movie about then. I will probably never know for sure, but the shoe fits. Mocked and ridiculed for his awkwardness and huge ears, Dumbo eventually flies and becomes the wonder of the circus.

I have always been somewhat overweight. I wore dresses from the "Chubby" clothing department, and I was awkward and rarely participated in anything athletic. My only saving grace in that arena was wearing steel-toed corrective shoes that helped when we played kickball in the street! I was teased by some others for being a fatty. "Joanie, Joanie, big fat pony!" was the cry. Today we would label this as bullying. This was long before "Plus Size" was an accepted label and body positivity was a movement of sorts. Have you read Alexander McCall Smith's book, *The No.1 Ladies Detective Agency,* which takes place in Zimbabwe? The main character, Mma "Precious" Ramotswe, is "a traditionally built" woman, a large-sized woman. What a kind and affirming term! I had no idea back then that, like Dumbo, I had the potential to fly!

I grew up in an average and ordinary suburban home in northern New Jersey. There was little drama and intrigue in the general flow of life. Certainly, there were the ups and downs of human conflict that weave through every group of imperfect human beings, but there was no abuse or violence or neglect or deprivation. My father was a hard-working man who diligently provided for his family. He worked blue-collar jobs all his life, and if he was laid off from one position on a Friday, he was working somewhere else by Monday. He might be digging ditches at a construction site until he found something else, but he still would be working. My mother was active with her three children's school affairs, serving as room mother or Girl Scout leader or on the PTA. I remember that the kids on the street tended to congregate in our yard because she was the nicest mother on the block. As we grew older, she held various part-time jobs to bolster the family income. We were never rich, but we were always secure in our home and were well-fed and properly clothed. No addictions robbed our resources or hampered our growth.

With this background, I am mystified why I sometimes,

in my weaker moments, pictured myself curled up in a corner with my knees drawn up. I was cowering with my head down and my face in my hands, wanting to hide, wanting to disappear for a while.

While I had trouble riding a two-wheel bike or competing in gym class, I did well academically and held leadership positions throughout my school years. Yet the reality of feeling shame would sometimes overtake me. I did not want to fail or to disappoint anyone. I was painfully aware of what I perceived as my shortcomings.

As I look back now from the vantage point of advanced age, I see some of the ways God has used these jumbled and immature feelings to prepare and provoke me to move into areas that are part of serving his purposes in the lives of others. Sometime in my forties, God painted a new picture for me where I am seated comfortably near him, sometimes seated on his knee, and I realize his intent to pour out his life through me to others who are curled up in the corner. Many of them have suffered with far more trauma than I ever dreamed of or experienced, but the grip of fear and shame that rises up like stomach acid and agitates the soul is universal. Most of my life work has centered on troubled people. Most of them were female. Many of them were in the context of dealing with upheaval and pain. Many faced unplanned pregnancy or pregnancy loss. I can see most of their faces and hear their voices. Many details have faded with time as the sheer numbers of people increased, but the essence of their stories remains. As I reflect on the many times I have prayed for them, I have come to the confident assurance that God will draw out of you and me—especially out of our own personal well of experience and relational pain—what is needed to connect to the hurts and pain in others. But first we need to see it and face it ourselves.

My own story is told with as much clarity as I am able to muster. I include it because I know that transparency and vulnerability are building blocks of compassion and empathy. While not everyone in pain needs to know my story, I need to know it at a deep level so I can walk in strength and integrity. We need not all experience the same events or traumas in order to relate, but the universality of human frailty and need is part of the core of being that makes us relatable. I also include my own struggles because they may possibly be helpful to share with some of the hurting people you care about. Henri Nouwen captures this thought well:

*The great illusion of leadership is to think that man can be led out of the desert by someone who has never been there.*

— Henri J. M. Nouwen, *The Wounded Healer: Ministry in Contemporary Society*

I am relating these stories as illustrations to benefit those of you who are helpers to hurting and needy people. You are called to come alongside the people God places in your path or sends you out to find. I hope this encourages you to keep on reaching out to others and inspires you to trust God to give you wisdom and insight that will help them move toward healing. Whether they need help with a problem pregnancy, a past abortion, a broken relationship, a fractured home, or a serious illness, people really do need people. As God heals you from the hurts in your life, he equips you to come alongside others. It has taken me a long time to grow into the person I am today, and I know God is not finished with me yet. I have outgrown many of my fears, even though some still linger. They will go, too, in time.

There are three things I hope you will know and experience as you read this book.

- You are accepted and loved by your Creator and by others.
- You are worthy and valuable as you are now and as you will become.
- You are uniquely called and equipped to help other people.

I have known and experienced the powerful and all-encompassing love of a tender and forgiving God. He has used the hands and hearts of many people in my life, and I have seen him transform others. My hope is that these true stories will help those who are still struggling in the midst of their own pain.

# CHAPTER 1

# My Father Will Kill Me;
# My Mother Will Die

*Shame can cripple us. It can also be the start of
building a bridge to freedom and fruitfulness.*

T he young woman shaking and crying on the sofa said
words that riveted me. "MY FATHER WILL KILL
ME!" she wailed. Breaking into loud sobs, she choked
out the words, "MY MOTHER WILL DIE." Sagging back on
the sofa, she pulled herself into a tight ball, hugging herself and
holding the positive pregnancy test in her fist as she continued
to weep.

It was not the first time I had met her. Back in October, a
call came in from a college girl wanting to make an appointment for herself and a friend. They both needed pregnancy

tests, and they wanted to come in together. We scheduled the two appointments, and they showed up an hour later. After doing the intake paperwork with each one separately, they insisted on being seen together. Giggling and acting silly, they explained that they had been best friends in the all-girls parochial high school they had attended. The nuns were very strict, and their parents were supportive of the regimen. Now they were at college together, sharing a dorm room.

For the first time, they were on their own without any adult closely supervising their activities. It wasn't long before they were invited to frat parties, and they couldn't wait to go to one. They had heard the stories, and they knew what to expect. The school was notorious for drinking, and the parties were wild. It was known that incoming freshmen women were "looked over like a new supply of fresh fruit, ripe for the picking—or raw meat, ready for consumption." These two foolish girls wanted to have their first sexual experiences, and they knew they would need to be drunk to have the courage to follow through with their plans. Easily obtaining birth control pills from the college infirmary, paid for in cash so their parents would not see the cost on a bill, they thought they were all set. By mid-October the parties were in full swing, and they were ready to implement their plan. Getting drunk was easy enough, as the kegs were flowing. Their invitations to go upstairs with a couple of the guys came soon after.

Here they sat, needing the support of each other to tell their tale to me, a stranger. With foolish but slightly sheepish looks on their faces, they never stopped giggling. They were given good information before the tests were given and made some slight acquiescence to heeding the concern about the risk they had taken. Basically, they were proud of themselves. They had "done it" and were no longer uninitiated virgins. Fortunately, both tests were negative.

As soon as they could, they made their exit—with literature in hand that they'd already seen and ignored in high school. I found the visit somewhat annoying, finding my irritation interfering with my ability to pray for them freely after they left. I felt that I was off my game and did not say anything that impacted them. Of course, I told them we were there for them and they could come back whenever they had questions or needed help, but I was frustrated by the sheer determined stupidity of what they had done.

The following April, Susan—the shorter one with reddish hair and sprinkle of freckles on her nose—did come back. This time she was alone. This time there were no giggles. Sober and scared, she went through the intake. She could hardly make eye contact with me, and her voice was almost too soft to hear. This time the test was positive, and her face quickly drained of all color. She slumped on the sofa as tears formed in her eyes.

Then she said the words that riveted me. Shaking her head and sobbing now, she said, "MY FATHER WILL KILL ME. MY MOTHER WILL DIE." She was not in a hurry to leave this time. Sagging back on the sofa, she pulled herself into a tight ball, hugging herself as she continued to cry. The bravado was all gone. The game she had played turned sour for her. Because she had become initiated into sexual intercourse, it became harder to avoid after the first encounter. She stopped going to the impersonal drunken frat parties but dated several guys during the year, who soon expected to include sex in the equation. She accommodated this as the reality of her adult status in the twenty-first century. Everybody did it, right? But everybody did not have to go home in six weeks and live in her house and tell her parents.

She had considered herself adult and liberated, now she had to face a decision about what to do. She was too frightened to even talk about abortion. That was another unspeakable thing in her family. Her cousin had gotten pregnant, but her "secret" abortion was soon found out, and she was the cause of shame in the family. Now Susan was in line to take her place, no matter what she did about this pregnancy.

Shame was washing over her in violent waves. She was the smart one. She was the "good" one. No, she was the phony one. She would anger and disappoint her father and feared his rage. She feared her mother's shocked sadness even more. This would destroy her mother's proud place in society, her leadership of the women's circle, and her position in the school association. How would she ever recover from this wretched shame?

I worked with Susan for a few weeks before she left. She seemed fairly settled on not getting an abortion and was considering adoption. The father of the baby wanted to deny responsibility and have no part of this mess. He knew he was not the only one Susan had been with, and he was not going to be the fall guy. I do not know the details of how this all worked out because Susan did not come back for her sophomore year.

One day the following November, I had another client react to a positive indication on a pregnancy test. To my amazement, she said the exact same words that Susan had said: "MY FATHER WILL KILL ME. MY MOTHER WILL DIE." Her circumstances and family background were totally different than Susan's, but the words were identical. The sense of shame was identical. It was then I thought this was a story that needed to be written.

The effects of shame are long lasting, and no one, I think, completely escapes the power of this shattering emotion. This book started to grow in my mind then, many years ago. I could relate to the awful feeling. Guilt is different and is stirred by the realization that a mistake has been made. Shame comes from something more insidious, from the belief that one *is* a mistake, a failure, a worthless being. I did not realize then that I was on the way to exploring shame and vulnerability in my own life and the lives of the clients I saw on a daily basis.

I have one outstanding experience of being publicly shamed. My husband was a naval officer, assigned duty on a World War II type submarine for a year of training. Among officers in the navy, attending social events was a requirement. It seemed that there were endless cocktail and dinner parties that often made me uncomfortable. I tried to make a glass of ginger ale last a long time as the ice melted and it became diluted. I was pleased when I discovered Bitter Lemon, a non-alcoholic mixer that improved in flavor as the ice diminished. Unused to alcohol, I would accept one glass of wine at a dinner party and stop there. If a husband had duty on the night of a party, the wife usually stayed home. One party was an exception because there was a baby shower planned for one of the wives. I was encouraged to attend with another couple.

The shower was soon over, and I was wishing I hadn't come. The men, about a dozen officers, stood in a circle in the dining room of the crowded house. Some of the wives hovered in the small kitchen, but most of the younger ones sat in the living room. I was just around the corner behind the men and could hear their conversation. The second in command started to tease the man who drove me there. "I see you have two women to handle tonight!" he crowed. Everyone laughed, and then he added a taunt from an old song: "Well, I don't want her, you can have her; she's too fat for me." The laughter grew louder as I simmered in shame and embarrassment. I remember trying to think of some witty remark I could counter with during the evening, but I knew I was too timid to challenge his insulting words. I was fairly sure none of the women had heard, but all the men had enjoyed the shaming joke.

I made my situation worse as the evening wore on. As we all sat around the living room balancing plates on our laps, the host kept filling the wine glasses we held. I drank too much and was drunk for the first time in my life. I knew it when I repeated the same questions I had already asked of the man next to me, a high-ranking officer who was a guest. I was quiet then till I was home, horrified that I had been so unwise and had brought inevitable silent ridicule on my husband. I did not tell my husband about it for a long time. At the next party, barely a month later, the host was the man who had insulted me. With a smirk on his face, he repeatedly proffered a tray of drinks that I refused several times before I finally took one and set it on the side table where it remained untouched throughout the endless, boring evening. Many would laugh at my immature concerns over the whole thing. I did learn three important things. I never again experienced being drunk. I learned not to venture into hostile territory alone. I also learned firsthand what it feels like to be shamed in front of others. That has helped me embrace empathy and compassion for those who struggle with shame in far more searing and sustained ways.

Contemporary scholar and author Brené Brown has made studying shame and vulnerability part of her life work. She puts it this way in her TEDx Houston talk, "The Power of Vulnerability."

> *Vulnerability is not weakness. I define vulnera-*
> *bility as emotional risk, exposure, uncertainty.*
> *It fuels our daily lives. After twelve years of re-*
> *search and professional experience, I've come to*
> *believe that vulnerability is our most accurate*

*measurement of courage. To be vulnerable is to*
*let ourselves be seen, to be honest.*[1]

Part of my personal struggle with shame is a sense of worthlessness that I believe relates to the strong influence my grandmother had on my life. I was my paternal grandmother's darling. It seemed I could do no wrong, and she lavished love and attention on me. She was not on speaking terms with a few members of the family, so some other cousins were ignored. All of her affection was focused on me, and I would go with her anywhere. I would spend week after week when school was out with her at the lake house cottage she and my grandfather owned a few hours away from home. My grandfather would leave for the week to attend to his business, but she and I had tea parties, made little pies with the berries we picked, swam in the lake, and visited with summer neighbors. We went back home several times, and my parents and brother came up for some weekends, but the long summer break was spent playing house alone with grandma in the woods by the lake.

Maybe I was five when I first remember riding in the back of the car, playing with my dolls, confused by the harsh dialogue I heard between my grandparents. They argued constantly throughout the two-hour drive to the lake house. Somewhat aware of their passenger, they did not swear at each other, but their words were harsh and biting. There was no kindness or

---

[1] Brown, Brené, "The Power of Vulnerability." TEDx Talk Filmed October 6, 2010, 20:44 minutes. https://www.youtube.com/results?search_query=brene+brown+tedxhouston+2010.

softness between them. If I interrupted with a timid question, my grandmother would turn and smile sweetly at me and softly answer. As I got older, I began to marvel at the contrast. How could she change tone and attitude so swiftly? How did I deserve such kindness when my grandfather merited such verbal abuse?

Woven throughout my grandmother's tenderness toward me was a strong thread of criticism of others. While she praised and pampered me, she shared her opinion of those of lesser worth. That included anyone of color or of doubtful ethnic origin. Those of other religious persuasions were always marginalized. If they lacked a British heritage or belonged to the wrong denomination, it was considered best not to become familiar with them. Grandma had good enough social control to act appropriately in public—usually—but I was her personal companion and confidante. I heard it all when I was young. Her words were confusing to me, especially as I grew older and made friends with many people she discounted. Years later when I was in college, I had a Kenyan suite mate. When I asked to bring her home for a holiday break, permission was denied. My father was concerned about the storm that would raise with my grandmother, who lived just across the street.

If I was so special, why was everyone else deemed inferior? I remember feeling like I was a phony, a false and hollow image. As my worldview expanded and I made friends with those my grandmother rejected, I struggled with eliminating the negative weeds that were planted right beside the tender blooms that surrounded me.

Our idyllic summers ended when I was eleven. I knew something was going on and was aware that Grandpa's business was failing. I was already in bed one evening when Grandma came into my room to tell me the lake house was sold. I cried myself to sleep that night and several others after that. We still saw much of each other because of our close proximity.

My grandparents made an apartment in the attic of their small brick bungalow, added an outside stairway to it, and rented it to a single woman. After Grandpa died when I was away at college, Grandma sold the house with the condition that she could rent the apartment for herself. It always seemed so sad to me. Whenever I was home, I would go and visit her in her one-room place with the tiny kitchen and bathroom. We would have tea and cookies, like old times. Of course, it was never really the same. The child and the adult had gradually changed places over the years.

As I crossed the bridges that gradually moved me away from shame and fear, I began to see how many others suffered in the same way. This transformation prompted me to reach out and relate to other vulnerable people I met along the way.

# CHAPTER 2

# Guilt and Grace

*Guilt can drive us to self-destruction or
lead us to a new level of maturity.*

M ike arrived looking very distraught. He plopped down on the sofa in my room and started talking before I could introduce myself and welcome him. "My girlfriend is pregnant, and we have an abortion scheduled for tomorrow. I am going to go straight to Hell!" Hanging his head in his hands, he said that if their parents found out, they would both be in big trouble. Both sets of parents were active in a large pro-life organization and worked diligently to oppose all abortions. The young couple had met as they worked on fundraisers alongside their parents. They started dating when they were in college, and their parents had no idea they had started having sex. They would be livid if they found out that there was a pregnancy, but they would go ballistic if they knew about an abortion.

As he rambled on about the situation, Mike began to calm down. He knew all the statistics, he knew the risks of abortion, and he was well versed in the value of human life. But this was suddenly about *his* life and *his* future. Neither he nor his girlfriend were ready for a child now. They both had two-and-a-half years of school left, at a minimum. Plans for the future were still forming as they explored careers and graduate training. Their hopes were high and certainly did not include dropping out to raise a family. In his miserable frustration, he was too boxed in to think of workable alternatives and too overwhelmed by the prospect of facing the virulent rebuke he would surely receive. Although they both felt guilty for their actions, his training taught him that he was the one needing to take primary responsibility for the mess they were in. Now they were very close to making the mess far worse and producing more guilt for both of them. It would humiliate their parents and drive the two of them apart inevitably. They just knew an abortion violated their own convictions.

When Mike left, he promised to return in the morning with his girlfriend a few hours before the abortion was scheduled. They did come in, and she looked more forlorn than Mike. It turns out that the woman who originally sent them to the pregnancy center did not share the ethic of preserving their privacy, and she had already called the parents and told them the situation. I am not sure how she found out in the first place, but she was determined to thwart the abortion. Instead of heading to an abortion clinic later that day, they would be heading to a tense family pow wow, and they dreaded it.

The brief time they spent with me focused on the benefits of being honest with themselves and with their parents. We spoke about looking at their situation by carefully taking one step at a time and letting everyone cool down. What decisions needed to be made immediately? Now that their parents knew about the pregnancy, there was no need to try to bury their guilt by getting a hasty abortion that would only magnify it and complicate the problem. Parenting and adoption options could both be reviewed at a later time. Schooling could be continued at least through the end of the semester. *Prioritize the order,* I counseled. Unpack one bag at a time as things begin to be sorted out.

I offered follow-up help for them and their families if any of them wanted to talk. I never saw them again, and I do not know exactly how things ultimately resolved, but I did hear through the informant that they did NOT get an abortion.

There are some who say people only feel guilt when others express disapproval of some of their choices and try to make them feel guilty. I believe we all have a moral compass of some sort, buried deep within perhaps, made up of attitudes and influences and beliefs we have carried over the years. Denying those inner promptings can lead us into peril if we do not honestly look at them, seek out comprehensive information, and move with sincere conviction and a willingness to bear the long-term consequences of our decisions.

I do not think these two young people would have survived as a couple if they covered their unplanned pregnancy with an abortion. It would not have been acceptable for me to have pushed my way into their lives and informed others of their situation, but someone in their pro-life circle did upset the apple cart. My call was to speak truth, listen to their venting, and move them toward an honest assessment of their circumstances. I would want them to own their choices, face the anger and disappointment of their families, and make a plan for their future and the future of the child they were carrying. I believe that these steps would have helped them the most to step into adult responsibility and resolve the guilt load they were carrying without adding immeasurably to it. The psalmist and king, David, expresses it this way:

*My guilt has overwhelmed me like a burden too heavy to bear.*

— Psalm 38:4 (TPT)

I thought of another couple I knew. They had slipped into a sexual encounter and conceived a child against their better judgment. Truly caring for each other, they were devastated by their actions. Almost their whole college career lay ahead of them, and the thought of giving that up now was overwhelming. They both informed their parents and made a clear decision to place their child for adoption and also place their relationship on hold. I met with the young couple and also met with her parents. There was grace abounding in this family. The young people not only truly cared for each other but also felt tenderly toward their unborn child.

After much careful consideration, the young woman's parents stepped forward with a plan for the adoption of their own grandchild. This completely freed their daughter and the young man to move forward with their career plans and did not force them to push their relationship forward into premature permanence. The plan would make it possible for both of them to see and know their child as he grew up in a close family relationship, and there were no strings attached that might hinder their future career plans. Over time, the couple did accomplish their educational goals and laid the foundation for a healthy life together. Eventually they married, the adoption was reversed, and they are now raising their son and his siblings with the ongoing blessing of close grandparents nearby. Truth-telling, love, and wisdom turned a nightmare into a win-win realization of a dream. Making mistakes is a part of life that we all encounter and have to deal with. Some are serious, and some are life threatening. Some are simple and need to be turned around, and some become so complicated that they lead down a frightful path.

> *Then I finally admitted to you all my sins, refusing to hide them any longer. I said, "My life-giving God, I will openly acknowledge my evil actions."*

*And you forgave me! All at once the guilt of my sin
washed away and all my pain disappeared.*

— Psalm 32:5 (TPT)

Self-focused guilt often stems from our own insecurities and concerns about our failures. This can make us pile up regrets that no one else may notice or know about. We think wrong thoughts, and it can make us judge others inwardly while we smile on the outside, feigning agreement or approval. I noticed recently that when I check into a social media site to scan personal news, I automatically pass over a few particular contacts. I am put off by their self-promotion and self-aggrandizement. I could just unfriend them and save the time of going down the list, but that offends something in me. It is not their fault. First, I need to look for the source of my own critical thoughts. Then I need to empathize with the need they are expressing as they draw attention to themselves. Maybe then there is a way to reach across the miles and affirm them in a new way.

Understanding of right and wrong is deeply imbedded in most emotionally healthy people. What have we been taught? What have we seen or heard? What have we incorporated into our belief system, and by what authority are we led? Most religions teach some sort of instructive code. Agnostics and atheists I know also hold to inner codes that shape their actions and thoughts. Christians turn to the Bible for a comprehensive understanding of right and wrong, how to set up a legal system, and how to form healthy relationships. Even as cultural changes occur and behavioral mores shift, some fundamental patterns prevail.

True guilt is different than guilty feelings. It is a gift. It stands right in front of us and makes us pause and take a look. It pushes buttons that force us to become uncomfortable and slow down. Why did I do that? Surely, I knew better. What am I trying to prove, and to whom? If I do not acknowledge my own guilt issues, how may I be equipped to observe and unpack guilt issues with others?

I remember a time as a child when I deliberately chose to do something wrong. I damaged the newel post, the final post at the bottom of the stairway, and let my older brother take the blame. Years later I wrote this about the experience:

## The Newel Post

*What made me damage the newel post so deliberately? I stood there idly with a knife in my hand and repeatedly scored nicks down the length of one edge. They were thin shallow cuts, hard to see but rough to the touch. I don't remember how old I was when I did it. It was weeks or months later before anyone discovered the damage. One day my older brother was standing on the second step, and I stood at the bottom. Mom was agitated about something long lost to memory, but I remember*

*the feeling of tension over her annoyance around*
*something she was talking to us about. Then her*
*hand rested on the scarred post, and she stooped to*
*examine the abrasive surface she had just discov-*
*ered. "Who did this?" she shouted. She looked at*
*my brother accusingly. I never fell under her gaze.*
*I was the "good" child. I didn't do mischievous*
*things. This was typical of the type of thing my*
*brother might do. He shrugged his shoulders and*
*said he didn't remember but easily agreed it was*
*probably his handiwork. My mother's anger was*
*quickly diffused, and the incident was dropped*
*without further repercussions. I remembered it*
*decades later and told my brother at some fam-*
*ily gathering, but he had long forgotten it. I had*
*stood there and let my brother absorb the blame*
*for my foolishness, intent on preserving my image,*
*retaining my status, perhaps trying to convince*
*myself and God that I really was the "good" child.*

As a younger teenager, I began to seriously explore my
Christian heritage. By God's good grace, I came to a place of
personal faith in Jesus Christ. The baggage I brought with me
was hard to leave behind. I wrestled with the fear that I was
not worthy, that I would never be good enough to please God
or anyone else. Grandma had me on a pedestal, and I had accepted her adulation for a long time. She was even delusional

enough to suggest that I would be a debutante and be presented to Queen Elizabeth.!

As I learned of my need for forgiveness and salvation, I had to face my own sin. The honey I was fed when I was little stood in sharp contrast to the reality of what I saw within me and around me. I needed to be cleansed of the negative attitudes that seeped into my pores and coalesced with the basic selfishness of my own nature. There was little drama in my life in these years, but the cloak of niceness that I inherited so easily could not cover the things that I battled with on the inside.

As I think about Grandma, I look back over the years tutored by the lessons of life and love so generously given by a loving God. I realized that she was a victim of her own fears, ingrained in her by others before her. I would love to put my arms around her now and tell her not to be afraid—not to be afraid of those who are different or foreign or better educated or socially advanced or in poverty or sick. I tried to tell her at her bedside in the hospital that she has nothing to prove to a God who knows every thought and feeling she ever had and still calls her by name. I trust she knows that now and rests in his care. My hope is that we will have tea again someday, when we are both all grown up.

Lauren Daigle's hit single "You Say"[2] stayed on the top of Christian music charts for over 100 weeks, breaking records for a female artist. The song repeats in my mind, reminding

---

[2] Daigle, Lauren. "You Say." Uploaded August 8, 2018. https://www.youtube.com/watch?v=N8WK9HmF53w

me that it is what God says about someone that really matters. Like so many others, and I think especially so for women, I have often sagged under the weight of what others think and may believe about me. I allowed their thoughts and behaviors to become, in my own mind and heart, lies that said I was an unworthy failure. It has taken years of growing up to come closer to the truth that God created me to be loved and to love others. Perhaps the words of her song will expose lies you may be hearing and believing—lies that are keeping you from hearing and receiving the peace and freedom you need to be all God has made you to be, with the capacity and courage to do all that he has called you to do.

# CHAPTER 3

# Please, Just Listen

*Deep listening is the first step to unlocking*
*heart-to-heart communication.*

E llen pulled into the parking lot in an expensive little sports car. She had called to come in and talk to someone about an abortion she had a few months ago. The receptionist greeted her and let me know she was there. In the few minutes it took me to end my phone call and come out to greet her, Ellen had picked up a book from a donated stack that had been carelessly placed on a shelf in the waiting room the day before and had not been sorted or approved yet. I think the title was *Enemies of Choice*, and it pricked her attention. I greeted her and told her my name. Her first words were, "I think I might be in the wrong place." I suggested that we meet in my office for a while and if she decided she was in the wrong place, she could leave at any time.

She took a seat in the armchair and crossed her arms tightly over her chest and looked steadily at me. "I am an atheist, a feminist, and a socialist," she stated. I nodded my head and smiled and said, "I am a Christian. I'm OK with you. Are you OK with me?" She paused a moment, visibly relaxed, and began telling me her story.

Her family lived in the next county where both of her parents were professors at a large university. They had scores of intellectual friends and hosted guests frequently for lavish parties and literary salons. They were enlightened and tolerant and counted people from many ethnic and racial groups among their acquaintances.

Ellen was the youngest of three children, and the others were already on their own. She had always been given lots of freedom to do as she pleased and become whatever she wanted. She had gotten pregnant at the end of her freshman year at a distant university. She told her parents easily and suggested that she might like to keep the child. It was no surprise to them that she was having sex. They had prepared her for that. Keeping the child was a more serious matter. She had obviously not been careful about birth control, and that was a disappointment. They had not met or even heard of the young man who fathered the child, and there were discussions about his suitability and ability to raise and support a child. There were strong hints that college would be over for her since they did not intend to support her financially if she went down this path. That was the first upset.

As things unfolded and the boyfriend was asked to come for a visit, the other shoe dropped. He was from a poor neighborhood in LA, attending school on a minority scholarship. It was one thing to befriend and even have a fling with a black man, but to bring a mixed-race child into this family would be unheard of. It simply was not to be allowed. Egalitarianism and tolerance had its limits, and she had crossed the line. Ultimatums were made, and Ellen was soon off to the abortion clinic. Now, as the time approached for her to return to school, she wanted to talk about it.

Talk she did. It was difficult to say much as she talked at length. I listened intently, asked some open-ended questions, and listened some more. She was quite loquacious and rather eloquent as she reviewed her youthful dreams and assumptions and explored the disappointments she was experiencing as she started to stumble into adulthood. I prayed for her silently as she talked, asking God for direction, as I listened without breaking the communication with her. The hour was quickly over, and she asked if she could come again the next week. She thanked me and left, briskly off to her next activity.

The following week was similar to the first. She enjoyed talking again. She did not take notes and was surely not recording my remarks because there were so few. Aside from some reframing and exploratory statements, I again was the listener. It seemed cathartic for her to review the details of her situation and to sort out her jumbled feelings. Why were her parents so strong about promoting their enlightened ideas and yet so closed about actually implementing them? What did her freedom of choice mean to them while they were the ones exercising power over her decisions?

Near the end of the time, she paused and said she would not be able to come in again because she was leaving at the end of the week to return to school. "I really want to thank you," she said. "You listened to me. My mother never listens to me, but you really listened to me." We shook hands and she was quickly gone. I welcomed her to come back whenever she was home again and gave a referral to a center near her school.

I never saw or heard from her again. I have thought about the visits and prayed for her over the years. I have no way of assessing the true impact of the time together, but this I do know. This young atheist with free-thinking ideas sat for two hours with an admitted Christian and was acknowledged and respected. I wonder where that seed landed?

If you want to be with other people in a helping mode, I think you should learn to wear "an invisible key" on a chain around your neck. This figurative key would never be seen but would always be available for use. It is the key that opens up the power of listening. Learning to listen is foundational to any attempt to cause meaningful change in a relationship. Listening skills are a necessary element of basic training for counselors and are also needed in any other endeavors to become effective when working with others. You know what it is like to have a medical provider with a "good bedside manner." Your favorite teachers not only communicated subject matter effectively but also heard your responses. Your true friends are the ones who actually hear you, both the content of what you say and the emotion with which you express it. A wise and tender parent knows just when to tickle or tease you, read you a story, or hold you and rub your back because they are listening to the messages you are sending subliminally.

One of the chief hurdles to overcome in listening is the pattern we almost always fall into that causes us to try to frame what we are going to say in reply to someone else, even before they finish speaking. We want to say caring things, helpful things, wise things. While our minds are trying to sort that out, we miss the clues and the pathos in the messages being sent to us. We leap to premature conclusions and make assumptions. We may interrupt, without permission, and start to speak in order to express what we have been processing in our own mind. Another common hurdle in listening is the failure to use silence. Silence is a critical part of healthy and productive conversation. It's not just "wasted time." It gives people an opportunity to think and process what they have been listening to. It gives them an opportunity to think about what they have and are willing to contribute to the conversation.

Not every person talks non-stop like Ellen did. One of my counseling friends spent almost a whole hour with a timid young woman who was afraid to speak. The counselor made some introductory comments, mentioned some of the things they could talk about, and offered to wait till the woman was ready. Confident and relaxed, the counselor prayed silently with her eyes open, reviewed some notes for an article she was writing, and occasionally made an encouraging remark. As the end of the hour drew near, when the woman expected her mother to come for her, she suddenly began to cry and blurted out her troubles. It would have been easy to wrap up the session much earlier, tell the woman to sit in the waiting room, and not "waste the time." It was the first of a long string of effective counseling sessions that followed weekly. Listening and "wasting time" waiting for someone else to speak is a powerful tool for real communication, both in one-on-one conversations and in larger group settings. Deep listening is a skill that can be learned. Business coach and psychiatrist Mark Goulston, MD, expresses it this way in his book, *Just Listen: Discovering the Secret of Getting Through to Anyone*.

> *Two things that I've learned from my own experience. The first is that simply listening to people will change both their lives and yours. And the second is that nearly all people—no matter who they are and where they live—will respond to true, agenda-less listening in an authentic and heartfelt way.*[3]

It is a challenge to put our agenda aside and hear—truly

---

[3] Goulston, MD, Mark. *Just Listen: Discovering the Secret of Getting Through to Anyone*. New York: Amacom, 2010.

hear—someone else. We have probably all played this game at a party. Something is whispered to the first person in a circle and then "whispered down the lane" to each person in order. What is said by the last person is seldom even similar to the original message. It is funny in a game, but it is not funny when someone's life story is being poured out before you. Married couples, parents and children, and work colleagues can be together for years and yet not really know what each other thinks and feels. Use that magic key to unlock your powers of concentration and empathy. You will be amazed by how much you learn.

# CHAPTER 4

# Abandoned

*Abandonment sabotages well-
formed hopes and dreams.*

ear the end of an appointment-filled day, someone
called for a pregnancy test. No volunteers were available, so I made space for one more meeting myself. I
had just a few minutes to peruse the information gleaned from
the phone call. Nothing seemed out of the ordinary. She was
concerned, worked nearby, and would come alone. One might
be tempted to use the word "routine."

I greeted Tara with a smile and a handshake, noticing her
stylish outfit and impeccable manicure. She sat with relaxed
grace in the armchair, poised enough for portrait photography,
I thought. She smiled appropriately and answered questions
confidently. When I inquired about her partner's involvement,

a shadow of fear darkened her eyes momentarily. It was the first visible flaw in her seemingly impenetrable armor of charm. She said she would prefer to have the test before she talked about him. I set up and explained the self-administered test, which she performed with only a slight tremor in her hand. In a few minutes she read the negative indication with a combination of disbelief and relief. Like a sudden storm sweeping tumultuous clouds racing across a summer sky, I watched her composure begin to twist and break apart. She slumped in her chair and stifled a sob. With painful intensity, she told her story.

"He left," she said. "We were together over three years, and we both knew it was over. He took a job in Texas, and we agreed to end it. But he was lonely and begged me to come and see him. We had another week in the sun, and I began to hope we could make it work. His calls ceased soon after I returned home. He began to meet people there and didn't need me anymore." Steadying her voice, she looked at me and said, "If I were pregnant this time, I'd have the baby. I've had two abortions to try to keep us together. I cry alone at night, hating myself for what I have done and hating him for not stopping me."

Tara left that day with an appointment scheduled for post abortion counseling. She said it was the first time she had revealed her frightening secret, the first time she had any hope there might be a way to recover.

Ordinary? Routine? Similar circumstances make it seem

ordinary. But being with someone going through such a situation is never routine.

Meeting many times with Sarah, another abandoned woman, was certainly not routine. She had also had two abortions before she came in for the first time. It did not surprise her that this pregnancy test was positive. Her anger spilled over as she talked about it. She felt so betrayed. The man she was with for all three pregnancies had reneged on all his promises. They supposedly had a very mature and egalitarian relationship, with ample room for open and fair discussion about differing opinions. They had discussed family plans but agreed to defer having children "for a few years." Their economic alliance was supposedly equitable. They enjoyed many activities, and both were prospering. They attended social events together to advance both of their careers. She expected a wedding soon and had begun planning a lavish event.

Now the relationship was falling apart, and many of her assumptions were dissolving. A third pregnancy pushed him over the edge, and he insisted on another abortion. There was no discussion, just angry demands. This time she refused and continued the pregnancy. Sarah was embracing a liberated lifestyle. She wanted to live freely without any barriers imposed because she was a woman. Now that things were breaking apart in her liberated lifestyle, the pain inside her had become unbearable. Her saga inspired me to write this poem, which was my attempt to capture some of the turmoil she was living.

## Equality

"I am woman," I sang, and I rode the wave
That was sweeping the nation like a newly found craze.
"I don't need enclosure in a girlish bower
Protected like some exotic flower."

"I am able, well able, to make my own way
Encouraged by sisters to seize the day.
I've found my stride; my step is firm.
I'm a self-made woman, and I'm quick to learn."

We shared the house for almost six years.
There were no obligations or whispered fears.
The mortgage was his and I paid rent—
No arguments there over what was spent.

The first time neither of us was ready.
We argued some, but our resolve was steady.
We each paid half, and he drove me home.
It shocked us both—my stifled moan.

I increased the effort to finish my courses,
Painted and cleaned, energy remorseless.
I gardened with fervor, row after row
Determined to make each vegetable grow.

*The second time I dallied longer.*
*The vague yearnings persisted, stronger.*
*He was traveling on business, but he paid the tab.*
*I went alone and came home in a cab.*

*The silence between us became routine,*
*Broken by an occasional ugly scene.*
*I was free to come and go as I pleased,*
*And he became restless as my ambition eased.*

*The last time he threatened to throw me out*
*Of HIS house, he would thunder and shout.*
*"I have rights!" I screamed, "and I've paid my share."*
*In his rage he said he didn't care.*

*Another has already taken my place*
*As he tired of my sad and frightened face.*
*I'm nauseous, exhausted, dangerously thin.*
*The child within—does it matter to him?*

*Alone in my room I cry in despair*
*With bitter anger choking the air.*
*I will not go back yet another time*
*To maintain our egalitarian mime.*

*"I am woman," I sobbed as I rode the wave*
*That was drowning the nation with a newly found craze.*
*"I need a partner in my pregnant hour,*
*Protected and nurtured like a precious flower."*

Many young women have hope and expectations for marriage and family someday. Many pursue education and adventure for a while, settling into a job that fills some goals and interests, but often with the intent that marriage and childrearing will follow in time. In most locations, marrying young right after high school used to be more frequent than it is now. I remember being told that a woman can't have it all. A career in a promising field and a fulfilling family life were hard to reconcile. As culture changes, that idea has often been debunked. I remember learning that you sometimes can have it all, but maybe not all at the same time.

As her pregnancy neared an end, Sarah and her partner actually reconciled. Her stubborn refusal to accede to his demands wore him down, and her swollen abdomen was an ever-present reminder that a child would soon be born. He gave up his dalliance with someone else and focused on the prospect of parenthood. After their little girl arrived, Sarah proudly brought her in to see me. Both mother and daughter were decked out in expensive outfits. She described the lavish shower that had been held and talked about the excitement of gushing family members.

Although I saw Sarah several times over the next few years and even met her son soon after his birth, she shied away from parenting classes and support group meetings. Her determination to make things work out well for her little family lacked, I feared, a good foundation. Her response to spiritual discussions was superficial, and I carried concern that things would veer off track again in the future. Prayer was my only recourse, and I prayed for her often. She knew there was an open door for her return.

## A Different Challenge and Opportunity

Maria was from Buenos Aires. She had trained there as a copy editor and was having trouble finding work. She decided to have a grand adventure and applied to work as a nanny for a year in the U.S. She loved the social life and was not sure she wanted to leave when her contract was up, but that was the requirement. Then her social life took her in a direction she had not planned to go. She came to the pregnancy center after she found out she was pregnant.

Her English was fairly good by the time she came to see me, and my Spanish was useful. We connected well and communicated easily. Her first problem was that the father of the baby was not at all interested in a permanent relationship, so he was not ready to marry her and sponsor her for citizenship. The second problem was that she was not really sure she wanted to make a permanent change in location. She missed her family and was looking forward to seeing them soon. She thought about getting an abortion and leaving this part of her adventure behind, no strings attached. If she kept the child, she would be back in Argentina many months before the birth. She could hardly hope to find a job right away and would need to live off the largesse of her parents. She knew there was social unrest in Argentina at the time and wondered about the long-term stability there.

As we met and talked over the next two months, many things surfaced. She was chagrined that this American boyfriend was so casual about their affair. She figured out that he got involved mainly because he knew she would be leaving when her employment was over, and it would not tie him down in any way. He accused her of deliberately becoming pregnant, "just to get her hooks into him." Ouch! That wounded and insulted her. She feared being alone and never marrying. Raising a child as a single mother would only complicate her future, she reasoned.

What also surfaced was the fact that she really did want to have a child someday. If she went home and did not marry, how would that desire ever be fulfilled? She had some religious teaching that troubled her, and she welcomed prayer with each visit and took a Spanish Bible with her.

We tried to unpack these considerations one at a time. Since she knew she had to go home at the end of two months, she wanted to be sure about the decision to carry or abort. She knew she would have to abort here since it was illegal at home. She carefully looked at the literature available and was fascinated with diagrams and pictures that showed prenatal development. An ultrasound, paid for by the center at a special rate, was offered at a nearby hospital, and an advocate from our center was available to go with her. She was won over by the reality of the life that was growing within her and decided to carry to term.

She wrote to her parents to tell them in advance, which allowed time for them to adjust to the idea gradually. Their tender reply encouraged her greatly. We helped her get to a legal aid advisor who had some family law experience. Since the baby was not born, no child support order could be initiated. She decided against pursuing this anyway, since the father was so defensive and would only make things more difficult. She said she would tell him when the child was born and wait and see if he ever wanted to know his child. I believe she was moving along and learning about forgiveness: forgiveness from God for the guilt of her mistake; forgiveness of herself for stepping outside of the boundaries she was taught; forgiveness of the father of the baby for his lack of care. Archibald Hart, psychologist and author, offers this word of wisdom:

*Forgiveness is giving up my right to be angry*
*with you for the way you hurt me.*

Maria flew home at the appointed time and was warmly welcomed by family there. She wrote to me several times and sent numerous pictures of her beautiful baby girl. The child is almost sixteen now and doing well in school. Maria will probably post new pictures when they celebrate the birthday. As of last year, she was still a single but content mother of one. Sometimes you only wonder how far the care you give can carry you around the world.

*To the fatherless he is a father.*
*To the widow he is a champion friend.*
*To the lonely he makes them part of a family.*

— Psalm 68:5 (TPT)

CHAPTER 5

# Help for the Whole Person

*The heart and mind are intricately entwined.*

M y family was living and working in an intentional community on a large rural property. A small group of adults and their children had come together to make a safe haven for people who were seeking answers and support for their lives.

Bev made her way to our rural group home setting. Someone had told her there might be a place there for her, and she wanted to give it a try. She had heard that a group was banded together with an educational and spiritual focus in an effort to help people find their place in life. She said she wanted to come alongside the eleven of us currently living there and see how she could help out.

Abandoned by her parents and rejected by a would-be

husband, Bev had fallen into a pattern of despair and self-destruction. Unable to find satisfying jobs and lacking many practical skills, she had wandered into abusive relationships and an unhealthy lifestyle. There was a sadness in her spirit even when a smile crossed her face. She was heavy-hearted, punctuating her quiet communication with frequent weary sighs. She never gave any vibes about being a danger to anyone and lacked aggression and energy.

As time passed, we became concerned about her increasing depression and the possibility of her being a danger to herself. A slow and steady decline was evident. Gradually she told us about some of her psychiatric admissions, and we were in touch with some of her former contacts as we sought additional care for her. Things started to come to a head before we could find her adequate help, and we started a twenty-four-hour watch to protect her safety.

The cottage we lived in was still under some construction, and there was only one easy exit for an adult-sized person, especially for someone who lacked much agility. I had the night watch, so Bev was sleeping in our living quarters. She was restless and quiet, but she did fairly well as long as our family was awake and active. As the children settled in and my husband went to our bedroom, I prepared for a long evening. The only exit was a solid wooden door that opened into our living room. Bev was bedded on the sofa, so I got some blankets and a pillow and settled down in front of the doorway. I could finally hear her breathing heavily, and I relaxed and let myself sleep, too.

She would have had to move me away from that heavy door to get out. I had carefully moved any dangerous objects from the kitchen area and felt we would be safe.

Several hours of good rest later, I stirred as the sun was slowly lighting up the snowy hillside with its brilliant beauty. I turned my head on the pillow and realized that Bev was lying down beside me, her head on the same pillow. I don't think she ever said the words, "thank you," but I felt the gratitude she displayed. She had made it through another night and, for a few hours at least, she was safe. Her inner demons had ceased for a while, and she could face another day.

Help was soon found where she could be cared for on a more consistent basis with proper medical help. I would love to say that the cycle of pain and disappointment that plagued her ended, but I do not know. We heard from her several times, but she never made it back. All we could count on was the realization that some good seed had been planted and she had a reprieve. I know the One who provides the seed, and my trust lies there. It is good seed and capable of amazing growth. We just do not always get to see what it produces.

Many years later, I met Gayle at the pregnancy center. She was sent by another client who thought she needed to come. She was hanging out with an irregular group of drug users, and they were all sharing a rundown house in the area near the train station. She asked for a pregnancy test as a way of having a rationale for being there, but it was soon apparent that she wasn't currently having sex with anyone. She had some disability insurance payments and saw a caseworker every few months, but that seemed to be the extent of her care. She liked to cook, and the others in the house were glad for the grub, so they let her stay.

Gayle quickly developed the habit of stopping by the center to drop off little gifts that might include some hand soap for the bathroom, a pack of diapers, or a sippy cup or new baby toy for the client boutique. Although not logged in as a client, she would often pass my office door and try to say a word or two. A regular cutter, she liked to update me on how she was doing and wanted to show me the scars on her arm. I got permission to communicate with her case worker, who verified her cutting episodes and her occasional psychiatric admissions. Eventually, she disappeared back into the system and was sent to a hospital on the other side of the state. Her extreme loneliness and obvious need tugged at my heart. I reviewed information on the whole self-mutilation phenomenon and felt better prepared to recognize it early. Sadly, it is not rare in the general population, especially in those who seek help from others.

Cutting, common in the psychiatric population, has also become more common in single Caucasian females in their teens and twenties, half of whom also suffer from eating disorders. Self-mutilation is the intentional destruction of one's own body tissue. In *A Bright Red Scream* by Marilee Strong, psychologist Scott Lines is quoted as saying, "The skin becomes a battlefield as a demonstration of internal chaos. The place where the self meets the world is a *tabula rasa* on which is displayed exactly how bad one feels inside." Neglect and physical abuse are often part of the history of the self-mutilator. There may never have been a secure attachment bond that helps a child feel protected, supported, and able to recover from trauma. Most people cry to release overwhelming emotion, but neglected or abused children often do not learn to self-soothe in healthy, socially accepted ways. In an attempt to release the feeling of tremendous pressure they feel inside, some will cut themselves and feel temporary relief, which may produce a sense of terror later. Since this is more prevalent among adolescent girls, there may be some copycat aspect to its frequency.

Trauma is pervasive and all too common. It affects people in different ways, but it is remembered in the body even if the details are lost to the mind. All ages, genders, and races are subject to its insidious influence. People are sensitive to being retraumatized through a variety of means, including abrupt removal from family, coercive practices, and harsh discipline. Sometimes invasive medical procedures that are intended to help cause a surge of bitter remembrance. Emotional or physical trauma can happen suddenly, perhaps repeatedly, and even intentionally. The person abused feels powerless to prevent it, especially in childhood. There may be multiple and overlapping causes.

Amelia, who was in an abusive relationship with a controlling boyfriend, came in for some emotional support. He worked long hours in an expensive restaurant and ate almost all of his meals there. He did not give her money for food, and he rarely brought food home. Her low-paying job ended when she was four months pregnant. She was estranged from her family who disapproved of the boyfriend, so she would not go to them for help. She not only lacked the cash for meals, but the manipulative boyfriend became angry and suspicious if he found food in the apartment because he wanted to know where she had gotten it and what she was doing to get it.

Her needs extended far outside of the bounds of the pregnancy, but we were faced with the fact that she was undernourished, and that put both her and the baby in danger. I never expected to have such a desperately hungry client. Finding money for food for her was not the problem, but she could not bring it into the apartment. As this unfolded during our first visit, I scrambled for something to do immediately. I had not had lunch yet, and I wanted to keep the connection going. So I grabbed my lunch bag and some extra things I had in the kitchen, and we sat outside at the picnic table under the tree in the backyard and shared some lunch. We went back inside the office, and I worked through referral sources for churches and shelters that provided free meals and made another appointment for her in less than a week. I called a donor who I knew would want to take this on, and she purchased a handful of gift cards for local restaurants so I could give Amelia one each time she came in.

Lunch with your new client is not in the training manual. It is not a recommended procedure, but this was a necessary life-line. We were able to move beyond that quickly. I am happy to say that Amelia began to face the reality of her living situation and eventually reached out to her parents and siblings. She left the boyfriend before her baby girl was born, and her life took a better turn. She became hungry for a better life and attended parenting classes regularly.

## Time Out From Storytelling

The following information is important for people helpers to know. I include it here in a change of format so you will be able to interact with it. You may want to move on past it for now; however, do come back and read it when you have finished with the stories.

### Adverse Childhood Experiences

An understanding of the powerful effect of childhood trauma has surged during the last decade as people became aware of the Adverse Childhood Experiences study. Before the study was done, children were generally assumed to be resilient and therefore only mildly affected by early trauma, or relatively quick to recover from it much of the time. News of the study's impact is spreading like wildfire across the nation and the world. Groups have formed in every state and many other countries to collect and dispense scientific information and implement recovery solutions.

In 1985 a doctor in San Diego, Dr. Vincent Felitti, was conducting an obesity clinic in the Preventive Medicine Clinic at Kaiser Permanente. He became concerned about the high dropout rate of patients who were, at first, successful in the program. He discovered through many interviews that significant excessive weight was often a coping mechanism for childhood adversity, often to escape fear, anxiety, depression, and anger. Many of those he interviewed had a history of child sexual abuse. This started him on a twenty-five-year journey of research and discovery to better understand the role of addictions of all kinds as coping mechanisms because of childhood trauma. Joined in the effort by Dr. Robert Anda of the Centers for Disease Control, they conducted a monumental study involving 17,421 participants. This was an unusually large cohort for such a study. They were all people who had insurance with Kaiser Permanente provided by their employers, which included an annual check-up. That made it possible to track the same people over a number of years. They had jobs and good health care. The original study included mostly white, middle-class, middle-aged men and women. Forty percent of them had a college degree or higher.

The study identified ten factors that were labeled ACEs, situations which cause health problems later in life, such as heart disease, cancer, addiction, and suicidality.[4] The ten factors are the following:

| ABUSE | NEGLECT | HOUSEHOLD DYSFUNCTION |
|---|---|---|
| 1. Physical<br>2. Mental<br>3. Sexual | 4. Physical<br>5. Emotional | 6. Incarceration<br>7. Domestic Violence<br>8. Substance Abuse<br>9. Mental Illness<br>10. Abandonment<br>(separation, divorce,<br>death, suicide) |

How many ACEs a person has accumulated before age 18 is predictive of future difficulties. Of the 17,421 participants in the study, 2,178 (12.5 percent) had four or more ACEs. Among people with zero ACEs, only 1 out of every 96 had attempted suicide. Among people with four or more ACEs, 1 out of every 5 had attempted suicide. Those with six or more ACEs died, on average, twenty years earlier than those with no ACEs. There is a remarkable link between the ten types of childhood trauma and the adult onset of chronic disease, mental illness, violence, or being victimized by violence.

---

[4] ISOSY has a helpful history of the original ACEs study in PDF format on their website for further study: https://www.osymigrant.org/ACES/Chapter%20Two%20The%20History%20of%20the%20Original%20ACEs%20Study.pdf

Published in 1998, the study underwent extensive analysis, and multiple follow-up studies and comments have been published. ACEs awareness gradually gained traction in the medical, psychological, educational, and social services communities. Other factors that cause toxic stress have been considered, such as bullying, racism, misogyny, war, and community violence.

I have not found a specific statement that connects ACEs to abortion, perhaps because abortion is considered by many to be a protected human right and viewed as a political issue. What is connected is the fact that risk-taking behavior is higher with higher ACEs. Long-term consequences of at-risk behavior leads to an increased incidence of STD infections at any time of life. It follows that acting out sexually at earlier ages impacts the number of unplanned pregnancies and abortions. What we are learning is that what presents as a problem may in fact be an attempt at a solution. We are all familiar with the statement that some people are looking for love in all the wrong places.

People do destroy their lives with bad choices, but what precedes that? ACEs lead to interrupted neurodevelopment, which leads to social, emotional, and cognitive impairment, which leads to the adoption of health risk behaviors. Parallel research shows that childhood trauma releases hormones that physically damage a child's brain and actually change its architecture. In times of danger, hormones are released which activate fight, flight, or freeze reactions. That is great in helping to react to a dangerous situation. But if danger stares you in the face night after night as you return to a threatening and violent home life, the body stays in the trauma zone and cannot go back to baseline. All systems are affected, including the neurological, immune, hormonal, and cardiovascular. The brain becomes unable to function properly and cannot focus on learning.

A thorough and readable resource on ACEs is *The Deepest Well* by Nadine Burke Harris, MD.[5] This pediatrician began to revolutionize her practice where she worked with disadvantaged children in San Francisco after becoming familiar with the ACEs study. She is currently the surgeon general for the state of California, and her goal is early intervention through identifying ACEs in pediatric practices across the state. Another powerful, and frankly disturbing, book is *The Boy Who Was Raised as a Dog,* by Bruce D. Perry, MD, PhD and Maia Szalavitz.[6] The case studies will startle you and distress you but will help you grasp the magnitude of childhood trauma as never before.

There is an online newsletter available for no charge. Formerly called ACEs Connection, it has been renamed PACEs Connection to reflect the more complete understanding that positive childhood experiences need to also be

---

[5] Harris, Nadine Burke, MD. *The Deepest Well: Healing the Long-Term Effects of Childhood Adversity.* Boston: Marine Books, 2019, New York: Houghton Mifflin Harcourt, 2018.

[6] Perry, Bruce D., MD PhD, and Szalavitz, Maria. *The Boy Who Was Raised As A Dog: and Other Stories from a Psychiatrist's Notebook.* New York: Basic Books, 2017.

considered. You can find it at https://www.acesconnection. com/. It will alert you to all kinds of groups and programs related to ACEs. There is a wealth of valuable information and much to ponder in each issue. One caution I need to share: Do not let ACEs become overwhelming or distracting as you serve others. The world is not shaped by this compelling perspective alone. Some very useful and truthful scientifically researched information can be forced through the sieve of a worldview with which you may not agree. You have the task of examining what comes through that sieve and pulling together the pieces that will inform your world and motivate your responses. The information gleaned from studying ACEs can be used incorrectly to discriminate and label others or to push certain social or political agendas. If it is ever used to screen people for employment, it would eliminate those who may become a future health risk. If screening becomes rote or is done insensitively, it could further discriminate or denigrate certain segments of the population. Do remember, though, that knowledge and understanding of ACEs can be a powerful tool to help see and better understand how to help someone recover from a hurtful past of trauma and victimhood or intervene early in a destructive situation.

I am pleased to see a new wave of research flowing in that emphasizes the powerful impact of positive experiences of childhood, which may indeed be more influential than the adverse experiences in many cases. Adverse childhood experiences are not new, even though the scientific study of them and their consequences is relatively recent. Throughout the ages, the abuse and abandonment of children has been a terrible offense to their Creator, a tragedy to families and communities, and the ultimate fall of nations and empires.

> *Jesus called for the parents, the children, and his disciples to come and listen to him. Then he told them, "Never hinder a child from coming to me. Let them all come, for God's kingdom realm belongs to them as much as it does anyone else. They demonstrate to you what faith is all about. Learn this well: unless you receive the revelation of the kingdom realm the same way a little child receives it, you will never be able to enter in."*
>
> — Luke 18:16–17 (TPT)

Is there an antidote for the damage caused by ACEs? Yes, there is great HOPE. I think the new emphasis on positive experiences will bring some better balance. God is always redemptive, and your past does not have to determine your future. There are positive and compensatory experiences that build resilience. Many sources speak of the restorative influence that even one caring person, one good connection, can have to overcome the destructive power of ACEs. When a person begins to find positive meaning and potential for good from a trauma in their life, then it is possible for them to move from being a victim to an overcomer and survivor. If God has given you a special burden for others, you can come alongside, alone or with others, and stand in the place where others have failed.

> *Ultimately, what determines how children survive trauma, physically, emotionally, or psychologically, is whether the people around them—particularly the adults they should be able to trust and rely upon—stand by them with love, support, and encouragement. Fire can warm or consume, water can quench or drown, wind can caress or cut. And so it is with human relationships: we can both create and destroy, nurture and terrorize, traumatize and heal each other.*

> — Bruce D. Perry, MD, PhD, and Maia Szalavitz,
> *The Boy Who Was Raised As A Dog*, p. xxviii

Encourage yourself with an inspiring story of resilience and redemption. One that keeps coming back to me is about Ryan Speedo Green. As a child, Ryan cowered in his room while his parents argued viciously. He was placed in a class for violent children and was eventually put in juvenile detention. There he was often in solitary confinement, and he seethed in anger. The book about his life, *Sing for Your Life* by Daniel Bergner, tells how he went from that situation at age twelve to age twenty-four, when he won a contest at the Metropolitan Opera and beat out twelve hundred talented singers. Now an established star at age thirty-three, the bass baritone is turning heads around the world. How did it happen? It had a lot to do with a couple of teachers who saw his love of music and helped him channel his anger into song.

# CHAPTER 6

# New Beginnings

*God can change any situation when someone*
*finds their strength in the Lord.*

W hen the marriage started to visibly crumble, the inner fault lines came out of hiding and began to be apparent in many ways. There had been deceit and verbal cruelty, and Carole was physically, mentally, emotionally, and spiritually depleted. Her former delight in beautiful things had led to an overwhelming collection of items that could not fill the holes in both her heart and their hollow and superficial relationship. Fortunately, her gentle nature and kindness to others had surrounded her with friends who stood ready to help her now in this time of crisis. She had a deep but challenged faith and tried to teach her children well, but they also were suffering and had their own losses and grieving to work through. It was a betrayal of trust for all.

Watching the whole household literally collapse around her was a painful process. It took many days and many hands to clear her house and her special places and dispose of the years of accumulation. He had already moved on and was making a new nest elsewhere with someone else. She was supposed to pick up the pieces, gather her chicks, find another place to live, and wade into the battle of the settlement terms in their somewhat messy divorce process. She felt shamed in a hidden, demeaning way. There was no yelling or violence, but she was wounded and bruised on the inside.

During that time, there were many small group sessions and prayer meetings in our suburban home and the homes of other friends. It was a change of seasons for me and my family as well, a refreshing one after our years of sojourn in country living and constant care of others. We enjoyed the comfort and relative prosperity of this new season of our lives, with good employment and much more relaxed schedules. As we had before, we continued to relish the close fellowship of people who took their faith seriously and wanted to serve others in need. It was a different kind of service now, without some of the poverty and drama and the severity of mental and emotional strain we had witnessed.

Human need surfaces everywhere, so moving back to the suburbs did not give us space to sit on the sidelines for long. The amenities were different, but the hurts and people needs were just as deep and widespread. We became members of a prayer and study group which met frequently. One couple opened their home so often that a week seldom went by without several dinner gatherings. Their door was, quite literally, always open. I dubbed that couple our 2:00 a.m. friends and actually was retrieved by them once late at night after my car broke down in the city while my husband was overseas. Carole was a part of our group of church buddies, and we all spent many hours with her. For the sake of the children, she cooperated with their father in many ways. Children always suffer from this kind of upheaval and struggle with divided loyalties. It was painful for Carole to have to make this transition with them. Time brought some healing as the children grew and worked out some of their grievances.

The most thrilling thing for us was to see Carole blossom. She had to tackle some practical things that had never concerned her before. No longer protected and supported by a husband who was a shrewd businessman with a high income, she needed to manage housing decisions and financial matters. Her natural intelligence surfaced through the fog, and her lack of much formal training ceased to be a hindrance.

Forbidden to work during the marriage, she and another single mother started and operated a lovely floral and gift shop that made an impact on the whole community. Many people were involved in helping it get started, and other ministries outside of church walls began to develop. The value of helping Carole and our other friend stimulated an expanded vision of service with a wider connection. People had invested in their lives and found themselves being transformed in the process as well. She found that to be one of the positive gains from her uninvited situation. At a church conference, she taught about some of the lessons she learned as she had to "separate the precious from the worthless." That applied not only to possessions but to plans and positions as well.

Since then, she has worked many years at interesting and creative jobs and lives surrounded by music and beauty. Carole continues to be a faithful friend to many people. She never married again or had another lasting serious romantic relationship and lives in a quaint house in a quiet town. Her garden is a wonder of delights, and her photos of its blooms grace her social media pages. Her home is again full of simple but treasured items, which are often given to others who admire them. Music students and children love to play at Miss Carole's house. She is aware of and caring towards her neighbors and keeps track of their needs and worries.

Her faith has grown sweeter and deeper, and she expresses the joy of the Lord through prayer and praise. When I think of her, my heart is blessed. I have seen what God can do to transform a wounded spirit into a beautiful and soaring being. Psalm 84 speaks of those whose lives journey through the valley of tears.

*Those who find their strength in the Lord, within whose hearts are the highways of holiness, dig deep to find a pleasant pool where others only find*

*pain. He gives them a brook of blessing filled from*
*the rain of an outpouring. They grow stronger and*
*stronger with every step forward.*

— Psalm 84:5-7 (TPT)

Going through the valley of tears and disappointment is not the end of the line when a heart yields to God's love and tender care. Carole used the tears from the outpouring to plant a garden. She said she "has taken those tears on mission trips to multiply in the nations," blessing women and children who are under-resourced.

Carole's story also reminds me of the need we all have for self-care. Carole grew stronger and more resourceful and productive as she learned to attend to her own deeper needs. Many times, self-care is easier for me to talk about than it is to do. Why not answer one more message or fit in one more appointment? Why stop for lunch when things are rolling along so well? A stepping-stone to disaster is the thought that you can do more than God is asking you to do. There will be times of stress and extra demand, when we push past our usual limits out of necessity, but we cannot live our whole lives that way. Rest and refreshment are part of God's design for human existence. We all know the drill about putting our own oxygen mask on before tending to even the children around us. If we don't, we may collapse before we get to them.

Consider the narrative of Jesus' visit to the home of Martha and her younger sister, Mary.

*Mary sat down attentively before the Master, ab-sorbing every revelation he shared. But Martha became exasperated with finishing the numerous household chores in preparation for her guests, so she interrupted Jesus and said, "Lord, don't you think it's unfair that my sister left me to do all the work by myself? You should tell her to get up and help me." The Lord answered her, "Martha, my beloved Martha. Why are you upset and troubled, pulled away by all these many distractions? Mary has discovered the one thing most important by choosing to sit at my feet. She is undistracted, and I won't take this privilege from her.*

— Luke 10:39–42 (TPT)

Carole is a musician and an artist who keeps music in her soul and beauty on her walls and windowsills. It isn't for the world's consumption as much as it is for her own nourishment. The thoughts and words of Rachel Carson capture this beautifully:

*Those who dwell among the beauties and mysteries of the earth . . . are never alone or weary of life.*[7]

Perhaps one of the positive benefits from the Covid-19

---

[7] Carson, Rachel and Linda Lear. *Silent Spring*. Boston: Houghton Mifflin, 2002.

Pandemic, which started in 2020, is that many people who had to stay home found or rediscovered pleasure in the things around them, learning to do something new or make something lovely, and listening and laughing more with the people they live with in community was a healthy and welcomed change. People took classes online, read some good books, and enjoyed bread baking and home-cooked meals more than usual. In the midst of horrific losses and disappointed plans and expectations, these rays of light were profoundly helpful.

There are endless articles with self-care tips, but they won't be of benefit if not embraced. People helpers full of compassion and empathy are sometimes slow learners and slow to initiate change. Deep breathing, simple exercise, and naps are great ways to slow the pace down and restore resources that will soon enough be in demand. Beloved Catholic teacher and priest Henri Nouwen modeled humble servanthood and spiritual devotion. He understood that the most important thing is allowing God to do his work inside us. When that happens, we are then able to actually do the work of God.

> *The question is not "How am I to find God?",*
> *but "How am I to let myself be found by him?"*
> *The question is not "How am I to know God?",*
> *but "How am I to let myself be known by God.?"*
> *And finally, the question is not "How am I to love*

*God?", but "How am I to let myself be loved by God?". God is looking into the distance for me, trying to find me, and longing to bring me home.*

— Henri J. Nouwen, *The Return of the Prodigal – A Story of Homecoming*

# CHAPTER 7

# The Impact of Abortion

*Abortion kills more than the unborn child.*

―――――――

Who is responsible for the huge number of abortions in the United States? How did it get to be considered acceptable and so easily available? What is its real impact in the lives of young men and women? The story you are about to hear and the specific quotes it contains are used with the express permission of the people involved in the story.

Rose was pregnant with her fourth child when she and James first came to see me. Referred by a pastor in the area, they were struggling but not necessarily because of this pregnancy. Actually, this would have been their fifth child. When she was sixteen, Rose had become pregnant. She and James wrestled with this frightening problem, and eventually the decision was made to have an abortion. They were not truly united about their decision then, and it was and remains an interfering shadow in their life together.

Most couples do not get this far. An early abortion usually blocks the development of a growing relationship. James and Rose's commitment and love for each other drew them on, and they married three years later, after they each had an encounter of faith with Jesus. Busy with family life and ministry work, they were hitting the barriers of regret and frustration that were causing them grief. What had been hidden and repented of—but not forgotten—was stirring them at a critical time in their lives.

At the time of that first pregnancy, James was stunned and embarrassed yet filled with urgency to care for Rose. He was ignorant about sex and how a female actually gets pregnant. He was a young college student and not too literate about human sexuality even though they were sexually exploring. He was embarrassed because his buddies would always look down in disgust at guys who would "knock girls up." He did not want to be one of those guys.

Rose was also naive and did not realize that her severe nausea was morning sickness. Her father had left home when she was fourteen, and she felt very alone. She did not want to further burden her mother and family, so her pregnancy was kept a secret. She was afraid and angry and sad.

How did they actually decide on abortion? They went to Planned Parenthood and were encouraged to choose an abortion, especially because Rose was so young. Subconsciously James was thinking, "If abortion is allowed—that is, legal—then it must be moral. This is America, and America is a good country with morally good laws."

James admits that covering his shame was also a big part of his desire for an abortion. At the same time, he was ignorantly thinking it was best to save Rose from carrying and giving birth to a baby at such a young age.

In more recent years, James said, "In deeper retrospect, I don't think I ever would have thought I needed a Savior if our omnipotent God did not allow me to kill someone in order to look good. The horror of this dynamic still haunts me. Yet Paul's words come to mind in this personal letter to his friend and mentee, Timothy.

> *Formerly I was a blasphemer, persecutor, and insolent opponent. But I received mercy because I had acted ignorantly in unbelief, and the grace of our Lord overflowed for me with the faith and love that are in Christ Jesus. The saying is trustworthy and deserving of full acceptance, that Christ Jesus came into the world to save sinners, of whom I am the foremost.*
>
> — 1 Timothy 1:13–15 (ESV)

He remembers being in Rose's house on the third floor in her room late one summer night when he was nineteen years old and saying to himself—no, not just saying but committing/promising/pledging in his heart—"This is my wife." No one but the two of them knew about the pregnancy. Rose feels she did not decide to have an abortion—she just followed what others decided for her.

It was twelve years after the abortion that they first sought help at a pregnancy center. Rose said, "It was only by God's grace that we lasted that long without help. There must have been angels on duty 24/7 to protect and guide us."

After that good start, they saw multiple counselors over the years as they lived in different places. More help and healing came through Rose's participation in a number of post-abortion recovery groups and then in leading many women through the same kind of groups for the next fifteen years.

James also spent time in a men's post-abortion one-on-one counseling relationship. For both of them, a weekend at Rachel's Vineyard, a post abortion retreat, was particularly helpful in healing and then strengthening them to move with Rose's vision of sharing their story with their children and with their family, which meant telling multiple brothers and sisters and their spouses. It was also there at the retreat during the memorial service that they named their daughter Cana Rose.

The abortion and sharing their experience with others had a huge impact on their lives. Rose says it has forever changed her. The abortion of her baby girl is her biggest regret and her greatest heartache. Neither James nor Rose considers this resolved in their lives. They are wonderfully functional as parents, grandparents, and homemakers but not yet resolved and healed as husband and wife. Underneath all of those functions, "in a subterranean stream, the abortion still carries the course of the relationship."

How do they see God's redemptive work in this? James says, "I truly see that an infinite being had to take an infinite punishment for me to be forgiven. I am ever struck with these verses in Psalm 49:7–9 as so resonant with my sentiments:

> *Truly no man can ransom another, or give to God the price of his life, for the ransom of their life is costly and can never suffice, that he should live on forever and never see the pit.*
>
> — Psalm 49:7–9 (ESV)

Rose says, "Raised as a Catholic, I thought I was a 'good' girl, at least my good outweighed my bad. The abortion dispelled that notion, and I knew I needed Jesus to pay for ALL my sins. Sad that it took the life of my first child to show me that even all my good works are as filthy rags. I am beyond grateful that Jesus' death paid the debt I could not pay, and that God's grace is greater than all my sin."

James and Rose have a long history of service to others. They have supported a pregnancy center for many years. Rose served on the board there for several terms, always striving to see the ministry grow and become more effective. She has led numerous post-abortion healing groups, and she is quick to offer help when someone is in need of that kind of help now. James has officiated at a post-abortion memorial service and has given his testimony at a fundraiser, helping raise money for the pregnancy center.

Both Rose and James admit that it has not always been an easy road. They are not the kind of people who have just varnished over their difficulties with a slick surface that can be removed with the scrape of a knife. They are real about who they are and know there are some more hills to climb as they grow old together. Their grown children have produced a nest full of grandchildren, who are the delight of James and Rose's lives. Approaching their fortieth anniversary, they can say with certainty that it has all been worth it, even though the baggage they brought into their marriage still weighs them down. They cannot say with certainty how things would have unfolded if they had kept their first child, but the faith that has nurtured them all along would have made a way for them with five children, too. They consider this resolved as much as it can be this side of heaven. James says, "Even today, though so much has been bitter, I adore Rose and am so glad I am still with her."

Living with the reality of a past abortion is a complicated matter. God does forgive even our most regrettable choices when we have asked for that forgiveness. He does it instantly and completely, and it has a powerful impact on our lives. Forgiving ourselves and those involved in the decision with us can take a lifetime.

It is all too easy to become critical of those who have

chosen abortion without knowing or understanding the circumstances which have led to that decision. It is too easy to pass judgment without looking into the mirror of our own lives to see what responsibility we have for making abortion possible in the first place. How many people echo James's thinking that if it is legal, it must be morally acceptable?

A number of years ago, I read a stirring book about the situation of apartheid in South Africa. I wrote a book review, which was published in the winter of 2007 in Care Net's *Center of Tomorrow* journal.[8] I have been given permission to use excerpts from that review, which will be of value to my readers and those we serve during these times of political, moral, and spiritual crisis.

In *A Human Being Died That Night,*[9] Pumla Gobodo-Madikizela writes about living through the horror of that time. Now a clinical psychologist, she is an international lecturer on issues of reconciliation who served on the Human Rights Violation Committee of the Truth and Reconciliation Commission led by Archbishop Desmond Tutu.

The author initiated a series of interviews (forty-six hours over a six-month period) inside Pretoria's maximum-security prison with Eugene de Kock, a man dubbed "Prime Evil" for his pivotal role as leader of the death squads that brutally took the lives of so many South Africans. Her account does far more

---

[8] Boydell, Joan E. Review of *A Human Being Died That Night,* by Pumla Gobodo-Madikizela. *Center of Tomorrow,* III No. 1, 2007.

[9] Gabodo-Madikizela, Pumla. *A Human Being Died That Night.* New York: Houghton Mifflin, 2003.

than draw you into a shocking and regretful period of human history. It telescopes you into her own soul as she explores, with disarming frankness, the depths of evil, remorse, forgiveness, and compassion.

She witnessed tears forming in the eyes of this criminal as he reflected on one bombing that left the wives of three policemen widows. This incident seemed to be one of the first times he connected with the fact that he had actually killed human beings. His voice breaking, de Kock stated, "I wish I could do much more than say I'm sorry. I wish there was a way of bringing their bodies back alive. I wish I could say, "Here are your husbands,'" he said, stretching out his arms as if bearing an invisible body, his hands trembling, his mouth quavering, "but unfortunately . . . I have to live with it." The probing analysis of the power and release of forgiveness—of oneself, of others, and by victims—repeatedly caused me to reflect on the process of post-abortion healing. If one feels remorse, how can one forget? "Look," de Kock said, you can do what you want, there is no way you can erase it. They may not be alive, but they are there. They are there in the day, they are there in the morning. They are there at night when the sun sets. You can forget about forgetting—it's like a daily calling card."

Like other authors who explore the moral choices people make, Godobo-Madikizela ponders the larger responsibility a society takes on when it sanctions or even encourages behaviors and then fails to protect people who suffer the consequences of those behaviors. When we fail to confront certain choices, that is a choice we make ourselves.

We live in a society that has legalized and rationalized the abortion of unborn children and even the sale of their body parts in the name of freedom. The definition of personal rights and choice has been expanded in a way that turns abortion rights advocates into crusaders with a misguided ideology. Those who promote, perform, and procure abortions are caught in the morass of an altered society they have both helped to create and become caught within. Who among us can engage that culture with truth that is saturated with humility, justice, and love? Do we, like Pontius Pilate, declare, "My hands are clean," as he sanctioned the crucifixion of Jesus?

My hope and prayer as you journey through this book—and this chapter in particular—is that it will challenge your assumptions about compassion and forgiveness and unsettle your private internal dialog about the courage of your own moral convictions. May such inner dialog lead to conversations with others that will make you a better informed and more effective God-led servant and caregiver.

# CHAPTER 8

# Help From Others

*God may use a team to get the job done.*

C ara and Brennan had been together since they were out of diapers. Their row of attached brick houses stretched the length of the block, with the backyard alley providing a runway playground of sorts where the neighborhood children gathered each day. Brennan hardly spoke to anyone. Following Cara around all day, she did the talking for him until he returned to his crowded little house when his father arrived home with his battered lunch box and settled down for a beer.

Both children managed to complete their basic schooling without any distinction or grand plans for the future. Brennan was taken on as a laboring apprentice with his father and was soon hauling brick and mixing cement for the construction crew. Working now, he had his cold beer each day too. Playing with sex began early as they outgrew more childish games and followed the natural order of things. With the first pregnancy, they married quickly at the parish hall, and he moved into her less-crowded household. Cara made a sincere attempt at parenting and came to classes at the pregnancy center. Brennan never showed up for any training, leaving that stuff to the women. With her mother taking some responsibility for the baby, Cara tried working an odd job or two to add a little income so they could try to get ahead. They wanted their own place someday.

It was less than two years before the second baby was on the way. Cara made her way back to the center, sometimes bringing her shy toddler with her. She came so she could earn supplies, and she came so she could talk to someone besides her mother. She lost that baby in the sixth month and came several times to talk about it. Her normal lack of enthusiasm dragged her deeper into a moody spiral of disinterest and boredom. Nothing seemed to stir her interest in any life bigger than what she had always known. She was pregnant again a few months later, and her second child was born at the end of the year.

Struggling with two babies now, Cara rarely made an appointment. Things were breaking down at home, and her father was less patient with this extended family to support. Brennan continued to work but spent more time with the beer and the boys and less time relating to his wide-eyed and fussy children.

After months without contact, Cara called and asked to come in. Her mother insisted that she come and drove her there to drop her off. Thin and shaking, Cara fidgeted with her broken and dirty nails and tugged at the scarf tied around her head to cover her thinning hair. Her teeth were yellow and pitted. It became clear that she was not eating properly, and what she did consume was soon brought back up with bulimic episodes. Terrified, her mother feared for her life with good reason.

Cara is the only client I ever drove directly to the emergency room. She was willing to go without a fuss. Although she had been referred for counseling through the center and also some social service contacts, she had never gone. Feeling helpless and hopeless, she felt she really had nowhere else to go but to come back to us. No place else kept the door open for her over the troubled years, and nowhere else was she allowed to try to talk things out without signing on for payments she could never meet or agreeing to leave home for treatments that would put custody of her children in jeopardy. Exhausted and confused, she agreed to go if I went with her. It was hours before she was admitted, but it was the first step of intervention that began to turn her life around. Contact was established with the hospital social worker and follow-up continued on both avenues. Professional credentials paved the way for this partnership, and Cara did not disappear into the therapeutic system. Her recovery was facilitated both by the medical assistance needed to save her life and the spiritual help and support from the pregnancy center. I had prayed for and with Cara many times over the years. Nothing ever seemed to have caught her interest or broken through her wall of self-protection. She carried on, believing that she was living a normal life, doing all that anyone should expect out of life, not looking for anything beyond what she knew in her limited sphere and saw all around her. It was not until life itself was truly threatened that she began to crack open.

I kept in touch with Cara over the next few years. The specific professional help she received made a huge difference for her. Early sexual abuse was identified, and some familial connection with eating disorders was revealed. She and her husband actually stayed together, and there were no more babies conceived. Most remarkably, she began to experience some steady sense that she had some value and worth and was able to set aside some of the unhealthy patterns that had weighed her down.

The range of "impossible scenarios" of people needing help seems to expand endlessly, with layer upon layer of difficulty compounding desperate situations. Since a pregnancy center is a frontline ministry, interfacing with the general population at a critical point of need, it comes as no surprise that it is a magnet for troubled souls.

Joy sat on the sofa with a strained look on her face that was punctuated with eyebrows stretched to the top of her wrinkled brow. Her naturally long face almost seemed to be extruded from her slumped shoulders. Her appearance was so incongruent with her name that she captured attention immediately. Pregnant from a liaison with a married man she had just met over the internet, Joy was faced with multiple conflicts. She had recently moved back home after her three-year live-in relationship had ended in explosions of rage and physical violence. Her complicated history included several psychiatric hospitalizations and extensive use of mood stabilizers and anti-depressants. She had a long-standing aversion to abortion but was being pressured to abort by the baby's father. Temporarily off medications because of the pregnancy, she was having difficulty at work just as her career was beginning to stabilize. Our client services director, a licensed social worker, walked patiently with her through the complicated process of finding the needed medical help for her particular concerns.

Psychological problems are married to spiritual problems. Counseling professionals who have a faith perspective know that one must address the issues of the heart as the key component to healing the troubles of the mind. Such appropriate opportunities are present in virtually every client interaction. Every day is undergirded with prayer, and each visit is viewed as a divine appointment.

The gift of presence, the profoundly simple ability to be with someone as they walk through crisis times, is one of the greatest gifts God gives to those who help people. The sacrificial volunteer service of trained lay counselors is a tremendous benefit for pregnancy centers. I believe there is need for both those valuable volunteers and for professionally trained counselors as well. Counseling degrees, like any other degrees, are merely one metric by which to measure one's qualifications. Who among us has not been influenced by the inspiration of a lay teacher? Who has not been comforted by the loving ministrations of a friend? Additional education, though, can open up possibilities to improve care in significant ways.

My father, who had a tenth-grade education and was a blue-collar laborer all his life, had a reputation for being calm and level-headed in medical emergencies. His ability to make quick decisions, muster appropriate help, calm the victim, and direct others did not grow out of any specific schooling. His skill was so obvious that he was the first one neighbors called upon for help. Perhaps that story best illustrates the relationship between lay (or peer) and professional counselors. Daddy could clean and bandage simple scrapes and cuts and dry my tears, but he knew immediately when I needed stitches and got me to the doctor in a hurry without causing additional trauma. A professional counselor is trained to recognize the need for more profound treatment. Like a good general practice physician, a professional counselor should also recognize personal limitations and know where to find the needed specialists.

Lay counselors may easily become overwhelmed when someone like Serena walks in. Divorced and hospitalized during her first pregnancy, she placed that child for adoption through a private source. Ten years later, she got pregnant again and sought help at a pregnancy center. Charming and manipulative, Serena was on social security disability because of mental health issues. So was her partner, Sam, who came with her for many of her visits. The combination was heart wrenching and ludicrous. Half again his age, Serena had used Sam to fulfill her wish to have another child, and this time she was determined to parent. She was also determined to get Sam to marry her. While Serena talked, Sam sat on the sofa nodding and smiling and chewing on the flesh of his fingers. Among other things, Serena exhibited all the signs of borderline personality disorder. She was ready to consume her counselor and the rest of the center's support staff with sweetly phrased but insistent demands for time and attention. Firm limits and directive assignments were needed to keep this one client from becoming a major distraction.

Every center should have professional resources readily available on the radar screen. Any of the following would enhance the outreach of the center:

Licensed Professional Counselor
Licensed Social Worker
Licensed Clinical Social Worker
Licensed Marriage and Family Therapist

Having such resources helps to build cooperative alliances with other agencies, which will likely lead to referrals from other counselors who are faced with a pregnancy situation with an existing client. That may provide the pregnancy center the opportunity to offer spiritual support to that client that is not available elsewhere. It also positions the center to be able to have interns from graduate programs because of the level of supervision provided. Ongoing continuing education course requirements for the professional are a rich resource for in-service training topics that can benefit the entire staff.

Licensed or not, client advocates with extensive training are keenly aware of the need for accountability to their peers or supervisors. Clear boundaries are important for the advocate and the client, and supervision focuses primarily on the emotional health of the advocate. In order to work with people at a deeper level, the advocate must stay aware of her/his own life and the impact client situations have.

Someone with training and experience with family counseling will enable the center to work with complex family situations. Family issues of difficult communication patterns and distress often rise to the surface when there is an unplanned pregnancy. The pregnant woman often becomes the "identified patient," the lightning rod or focal point of anger or shame in a disturbed family system. God often uses such a disturbance to realign the entire family constellation. The advocate has the opportunity to help pull the family back together after the crisis and guide them in restoring trust.

Rachel and Bill came to Susan's second appointment at the advocate's invitation. Although she originally considered abortion, Susan made a clear decision to carry to term and parent. Adopted herself, she was adamantly opposed to placing her child as her own abandonment issues resurfaced. Susan had a history of histrionic outbursts in the presence of her parents, and this session was literally heard throughout the building. It ended when she stormed out of the center, leaving her frustrated parents sitting in stunned silence. This was the beginning of many meetings with Susan and her mother and sometimes her father, too. Her parents came faithfully to a parents' support group run by our social worker. Susan was also seeing another professional counselor, and permission was obtained for her pregnancy counselor to communicate with him. Twenty-year-old Susan missed some appointments, occasionally failed to show up at work, and sometimes stayed out all night with her new boyfriend. Her outbursts lessened as her caring but demanding parents began to listen more deeply and give up some of their unrealistic expectations. They also began setting clearer boundaries for their troubled daughter. The involvement lasted well beyond the pregnancy as this family coped with the adjustment necessitated by the care of a newborn and Susan's eventual return to work and school.

As one counselor I know summed it up, the intensity of advanced training delving into the clinical aspect of meeting with another person promotes insight into life situations. Counseling is like playing a piece of music. If you take out the pauses, it becomes a different composition. Training and practice help one concentrate and keep the pace and rhythm with the appropriate periods of silence.

Another client, Marti, agreed to come in for some information even though her initial call was to try to obtain an abortion. She began to spew out her depressing tale of neglect and abuse at the hands of her alcoholic parents. On the streets by age twelve, she was working the dance clubs. Now a statuesque and voluptuous seventeen-year-old who had already had two abortions, it was easy to see why her sex partners easily believed she was in her twenties. As Marti recounted all the compelling reasons why she felt she had to have another abortion, her counselor, our social worker, resisted jumping in with ready answers, instead red flagging in her mind some specific comments for later discussion. It takes great control and obedience to the Holy Spirit not to go down every rabbit trail that presents itself. Marti said she had never even been inside a church, but that she was so fed up with her life that that she had actually prayed that if she ever got pregnant again maybe she could clean up her life. When her fury of words was spent, her seasoned counselor went back to that prayer. Marti made an almost instant connection, and the sudden revelation melted her resistance. She had talked through her own reason for avoiding an abortion and never went back on her decision. She had numerous appointments, eventually gave her life to Christ, and made huge strides toward a whole new life. She often thanked her counselor for listening to her so intently.

I would like to be able to tell you that Marti and her child continued to flourish over the years. The father of the child, a much older man, became involved and began attending church with them. They were accepted and folded into a small congregation with a sensitive and caring pastor. Marti's life ended suddenly under sad circumstances when some of her past began to haunt her. Her daughter continues to live with her father, and they are still surrounded by that unique church family.

Marti's pregnancy counselor poured many hours into her life, and Marti's greatest joy was giving birth to her beautiful baby girl. Her nascent faith was sincere, and I believe her Heavenly Father welcomed her to his presence with open arms, where her wounds were finally healed from the inside out. I think of the old spiritual, "Nobody knows the trouble I've seen; nobody knows but Jesus." His arms are the only ones that can hold that much pain. Sometimes, though, he allows us to walk beside the Marti's of this world as agents of his heart and arms. Only he knows the details or the final outcomes, but I find it amazing and humbling that he entrusts to such a person as I am to share the stewardship of the lives of others, especially as they go through severe trials.

CHAPTER 9

# Rescue Attempts

*Evil shows up in the midst of good intentions.*
*Be alert and active.*

W e were sure they were coming, so we all took shelter in our separate living spaces and turned out the lights early in the evening. The long driveway soon rattled with the churning tires of their speeding trucks. Everyone had been instructed not to answer the doors. Soon the pounding and shouting began. "We are here to get Sally!" they screamed. "Send her out to us, and we will leave." They tried every building, but no doors would open, and no sounds were heard. Sally huddled with us in our cottage, feeling both scared and excited by all the commotion. We assured her that we would speak with the authorities overseeing her care in the morning, but we would not let these angry people spirit her away in an explosive rush that night. After about an hour of yelling and clamoring, they gave up and roared up the driveway and thundered down the road.

It did not take long before the social worker showed up the next morning. He had been involved since school authorities had sounded the alert about the family. In this rural environment, many things were still done a bit haphazardly at the time. This was a most unusual family, with a mother and several children, all fathered by different partners. The latest partner was not the father of any of them but was a surly task master who pushed them all around. Sally was the youngest child and only girl. She was delayed developmentally and did not do well in school. School authorities were looking for a placement for her where she could thrive, away from the disordered environment at home. We were asked to take her temporarily into the home school residential setting we were operating. It was an informal agreement and not a direct placement, but it was set up by the social worker.

All was going well for a while. Sally began to relax and play with other children. The one-on-one attention she received with her studies helped her move ahead. She was a pretty child with a round pleasant face and long curly brown hair. Her mother came out for a visit, and I sat and sipped tea with her while we talked. She revealed, during that awkward conversation, that she was thinking about having twelve-year-old Sally "fixed." I think my jaw dropped in unbelief, but I tried to stay calm and asked her what she intended. "Well," she said, "being so slow, you know, Sally could never care for a child. She is pretty and men like her, and I don't want her to get pregnant." I did my best to counsel her that it was her job to keep men away from Sally. As she was a child, I urged protecting her as the first and best course of action. Inside, I was seething with indignation that such a plan was unfolding and became sure that some intervention was needed.

A few weeks later, Sally was scheduled to go home for the weekend. There was a family birthday planned, and all were going out to celebrate. When Sally returned, she proudly showed me the new dress her mother's boyfriend had bought for her. Long and lacy and sheer on the top, this black cocktail dress was totally inappropriate for a twelve-year-old. She described how she had danced in it at the party at the bar that weekend and giggled that a lot of men had told her how sexy she looked in it. I made note of all this and planned a conversation with the social worker.

It all came to a head about a week later. It was haircut time, and my husband was trimming hair for some of the adults and children. Sally said she wanted her long hair cut off. She had hinted that her mother might not like that, but then insisted that it would be all right. It had been growing long for quite a while, and she wanted it to be short, so off it went. She called and told her mother the next day, and that initiated the vigilante attack.

They said it would spoil her looks and make her look younger. They gathered their forces and said they were coming to get her. We told them to contact the social worker who brought her to us but feared that they would not wait.

The pieces fell into place. Pretty little Sally was part of an evil plot afoot in this sick family. It would not be long before she would be trained to do more than dance for the men at the bar. Child trafficking was not spoken of much at the time, but we believed that their intention was to profit by trafficking her as a prostitute. Since the placement with us was voluntary and unofficial, there was nothing we could do but air our concerns to the authorities who should be looking after her. It was the end of our contact with Sally, and we never really found out how the family fared.

A year or so later, I was in the town in the next county where Sally lived. As I stood on the sidewalk outside a store, the school bus pulled up and the students rushed off. Suddenly Sally stood in front of me, smiling and coming towards me. I was delighted to see her and was hopeful that we could speak for a moment. One of her older brothers immediately noticed and started yelling. She quickly pulled away and was swallowed up in the crowd. I was saddened to see that her life was still under the control of her "handlers" but glad to see her alive and going to school, hoping that someone was looking after her.

Sally would always be dependent on someone for part of her care. Either her mother, the mother's boyfriend, or her older brothers would be keeping their eyes on her. Whether by lack of protection or deliberate action, I feared she would be forced into some kind of sex slavery, either for profit or barter. I doubted she would actually be spirited away, but she would be unlikely to speak up in protest as long as she was given pretty things and allowed to eat candy. She liked to dance, and the bar scene was a likely venue. Much of the sex trafficking that plagues our nation and other nations is like that, in spite of stories that feature abduction and drama. Much of it happens right at home.

One quiet summer afternoon a walk-in client came to the pregnancy center. Our office manager was out sick, and I only had one volunteer in for the afternoon. She was busy with a client, so I took this new client. She seemed in a hurry, just wanted a pregnancy test, then had to be back on the road. Her father had driven her there and was waiting in the reception room. They looked very much like a father and daughter with their matching strawberry blonde hair. Both were polite and smiling, but something seemed off.

She gave a name and age, but I thought she looked younger than eighteen. They were travelling, she said, and had to be back on the road. I tried to make small talk and asked where they were headed, but she was vague. There was no address because they were moving to a new place, but she wasn't sure where. She had no identity card or cell phone, so there was not even a number where she could be contacted for any follow up. As soon as she saw that the test was negative, she was ready to leave. She did not want to discuss the father of the possible baby or any other concerns.

I worried that she was being abducted, probably by her own father, who might also be involved in a possible pregnancy. I tried to delay them, but they hurried to the car and pulled away. I decided to call the police and made a report of suspicious activity, even though there was nothing but a few details about how they looked and what color the car was. I could not see the license plate. The officer was kind and understanding but gave no comfort that anything would happen. We were near the state line, and they could easily have been out of range by the time the report was made.

It was a sinking, helpless feeling. I resorted to the only and best defense I had. I prayed for this mystery girl on her way to nowhere. I was reminded of words I had stored away for such a day:

*Put on God's complete set of armor provided for us, so that you will be protected as you fight against the evil strategies of the accuser! Your hand-to-hand combat is not with human beings, but with the highest principalities and authorities operating in rebellion under the heavenly realms. For they are a powerful class of demon-gods and evil spirits that hold this dark world in bondage. Because of this, you must wear all the armor that God provides so you're protected as you confront*

*the slanderer, for you are destined for all things*
*and will rise victorious.*

— Ephesians 6:11–13 (TPT)

If we are clothed in the armor God provides, we will not be overwhelmed by the evil surrounding us. While I may never know the fate of those two young women, the God of the universe does. He was and is able to use his warriors to rescue even the most vulnerable. Do not grow weary or be discouraged. You have been called to this work.

# CHAPTER 10

# Long Obedience

*Be open to but wise about long-term relationships
that go beyond normal boundaries.*

———

Shauna arrived with a harrumph and sat heavily in the chair. My smile was met with a wary and angry look, and she did not respond to any questions for a while. I took my time and chatted pleasantly about some of the things it would be good for us to consider together. She did not need a pregnancy test, having recently had one given by her doctor. It was her second pregnancy, the result of at least a second relationship. She took adequate care of her first child, taking her with her all the time, keeping a small and sparse apartment to shelter them both. The new boyfriend sounded like a some- what thoughtful and caring soul, but not one who would be easily tied down to long-term responsibilities.

This was the beginning of one of my longest counseling relationships. Shauna was not always happy, but she was always there. As time went on, she relaxed more and more, and everyone in the office eventually became accustomed to her occasional hearty laughter. Her needs were many, with a history of abuse and neglect that was years long. Her young daughter, Mandy, became the darling of the staff as she played happily in the waiting room or drew and colored at an empty desk. Special little treats and small gift items appeared from time to time, and her birthday and Christmas were celebrated in endearing ways. Shauna just fit. Many of the things she lacked through much of her life were being met through the circle of care and friendship she found at the pregnancy center. Finances were often a problem, but she always had food and shelter.

Chronically depressed, she had medical care through the social service system, and we weathered a few psychiatric admissions. She always landed on her feet, and a somewhat adequate aunt would step in to care for Mandy when pressured. Soon they would be back together again, struggling to make ends meet and carry on.

Some things just can't be easily fixed. There were periods of calm and times of storms. The boyfriend drifted away completely when the new baby was just a few years old. There was not a matrix of care and self-awareness that was solid enough for sustained and secure growth. Shauna did get involved in an inner-city church and had some genuine fellowship there, but I would still get desperate calls for help at unusual times.

Some things did change, gradually. I noticed improvement in Shauna's appearance. She began to care more about how she dressed. She worked on some secretarial skills and held down one job for several years. Her visits and calls were less frequent. The girls both grew and eventually launched out on their own. Just before I left the center to move on into retirement, I got the call to announce that Shauna was now a grandmother. She had found a new job, changed locations, and was seeing an older man from her church. I remember her fondly, thankful that the pregnancy center was there. Sometimes the touch point is not merely the assistance given during a pregnancy or the care that helps prevent an abortion. It is the long-term decision to be there for someone who needs a place to land, a place to stand for a while. It is a place where love is real and down to earth and not bound by artificial limitations.

Many client interactions are much shorter. A very sad young woman came in for a pregnancy test. It was perfunctory, really. She knew she was pregnant because she had been many times before. This time she really wanted to have a baby. Her first child was placed for adoption many years ago. She had no idea where that child was now. She would love to know but could not face the possibility that she would be rejected as a mother if ever she was found. Entering into deep depression and an endless round of drugs and brutal sexual encounters, Ivy became pregnant numerous times after that. Abortion was always the way out. The last few pregnancies miscarried before she got very far. A doctor sutured her cervix closed with a stitch, a cerclage, the last time she was pregnant, but it did not hold her uterus closed, and that baby's life slipped away early. Struggling out of the addiction, she tried to straighten up her life. This was the first time she had the courage to seek help at a pregnancy center. Her eyes pleaded with me as she said how much she wanted a child now but knew her ruined body would not be able to cooperate. I offered to meet with her regularly and help her through the load of grief she carried. "I was stoned out of my mind every time I had an abortion," she cried. Her look was unforgettably haunting. The next day she called and said she had lost that baby, too. I was hopeful because at least she called, and I thought she would actually return. I never saw her again.

Helping other people is a messy business. It is hardly ever work that calls for punching a time clock and going home. It goes home with you, sitting on your shoulder and troubling your mind with questions about what is going to happen next. I think of the difficulty medical workers have when they leave a shift, knowing that a patient may not be there, or even alive, the next day. When they leave, someone else takes over. Another nurse or aide checks the vitals and refills the water pitcher. Many times, I felt that there would be no one else for some of the people I knew. They did not turn over in a hospital bed to eat dinner, but they got off a noisy bus in the dark and walked to an empty apartment. They scrounged through mostly empty cupboards and opened a can for some dinner. Hopefully there was a can to open.

I had a long drive home every day, but most days I counted that a blessing. I had a family to return to. There would be warmth and light when I returned and food in the refrigerator waiting to be prepared. There was conversation and laughter, and someone who held my hand at night. I used the time in the car to sing praise songs, one of the rare times I could sing heartily without offending anyone's ears. It was also time to unpack some of the difficulties of the day, lay everything down for a while, and soak in some refreshment. Helping other people is a messy privilege; it is a messy gift.

On retreat with a group of women from my church many years ago, I took some quiet time as we sat around a campfire to write this meditative reflection on my life.

> *Lord, you have burned a long and steady flame in my life. You continue to consume the trash and refuse cast off by daily trials and sloppy sins.*

> *Your fire has taken the raw wood cut from stock of various density and durability. The pitch pine has long been reduced to ash, some still settled on the sand beneath the warming hearth, some long lifted to the winds and carried off. The harder stuff is charcoal, glowing softly and giving warmth for those drawn here, or ready to be carried to colder*

*places. Many live in frigid rooms, chilling places much in need of light and heat. The hearths are cold and barren, logs scattered in disarray, kindling lacking. Lord, show me where to carry my little pot of coals, willing to nurse a fire to life with hope and healing flame.*

# CHAPTER 11

# Unanticipated Blessings

*Good news arrives when least*
*expected. Celebrate surprises!*

---

The phone rang in the middle of the cold January night and was quickly answered by a bleary-eyed woman. Her husband rolled over and grunted with alarm. The caller was an emergency room nurse with the strangest of birth announcements. "There has been an accident. The baby is doing fine," she said, "but we are not sure your daughter is going to make it. Please come right away." They rushed to dress and stumbled to the car, flooded with emotion and confusion. The baby? They knew nothing of a baby. They had no hint of a pregnancy involving their youngest and only single daughter.

Linda was a first responder and worked odd hours of the night and day. She had moved into her own apartment several years before, even though she only lived across town. She liked this new step of freedom and independence, coming and going as she pleased, fitting a growing social life in with her hectic schedule. For the last few months, she had been talking about a grand holiday she was planning. She filled her schedule with overtime hours to save extra money and earn vacation time, making her presence during the holidays scarce. She would breeze into her parents' home to greet siblings and their children, laugh and talk a short while, and leave with a plate of food to eat during her next shift. She never stayed long enough to take her jacket off and relax a while.

Her ski vacation planned for early February was a ten-hour drive up to Vermont with "a few new friends" no one in her family knew. What waited there was not the ski slopes. There was an appointment with an obstetrician and an adoption agency. She had driven up twice already to work out the plans and choose the adoptive parents. She would go again a week before the baby was due and stay for three weeks. Even if she had to be induced, there would be time for some recovery before she had to return to work. Her one fear was going into labor early, but regular checkups with her local doctor so far had allayed her concerns.

There was no boyfriend ready to help her and ease the pain of relinquishing her newborn child. There really was no boyfriend. She was sure the casual hookup at a beer party was not the kind of guy she wanted around, so she never saw him again and never told him she was pregnant. Determined not to shame her religious parents or risk their anger, she spent the first several months after realizing she was pregnant working out the complexities of her plan. Abortion was a much easier route, she realized, but it was something she could not imagine. This baby had a right to live and grow up with a good family. One like hers, but not hers. Adoption was the only way.

The crash was a head-on, high-speed encounter with a drunk driver. Help came quickly, but it took some time to pry apart the twisted metal and get Linda out of the car. Some of her first responder colleagues recognized her, saddened to see her on the other side of the incident. Once in the ER, doctors swiftly assessed her pregnancy and did a Caesarean section since they thought they might lose Linda. Her injuries were extensive with complicated fractures and a severe concussion. She lost a lot of blood while they were extricating her.

Linda's parents soon arrived and were given a glimpse of the perfect little boy through the window in the NICU. It was many hours before they had hopeful reports about Linda. By that time, sisters and brothers, grandparents, and aunts and uncles were all huddled into a clutch in the waiting area. They shared their shock and tears and prayers for the young woman they all loved. They rallied like a cadre of dedicated soldiers, beginning to build a strategy of how to support her and provide for her child, their child, the newest member of the family.

Linda had never talked to a counselor about her pregnancy and had assured the adoption agency that she knew this was the right thing. She had never uttered the words, "My father will kill me." But she had known that her foolish and careless actions would wound this principled man and stir his anger. He had warned her about such things, had taught her right from wrong, and worked hard all his life to support his large family. She was the last child, the special and favored one in the family. How could she bring such a calamity upon him? She had never said, "My mother will die." But the tenderhearted woman who raised her was proud of her intelligent youngest and told others of her medical skill and training. She praised her for her selfless care of wounded people, sometime risking her own life in nasty weather to rush to accident sites or coming alongside of police officers at a domestic violence incident. Linda did not want to shame this tenderhearted woman with news of an "illegitimate" and fatherless grandchild.

A toxic mixture of fear and guilt and shame can lead us to tortured conclusions. Wanting to hide her transgression and protect her parents and avoid the full consequences of her life-changing experience, Linda had been ready to forfeit a treasure she could never regain. Had her family found out about her pregnancy in another way, there would have been tears and some anger and rebuke. Gossip would have spread in the extended family, but it all would have settled down soon enough. Adoption might have still been considered, but with greater counsel and care.

What Linda received instead was a groundswell of support from a loving family that was ready to put aside criticism and come alongside her to care for her and her son. They were not wealthy people, but they were giving people who could care for their own. And little Robert?

Surely, he was their own! He actually was credited with saving Linda's life. Doctors said that the cushioning of her extended and fluid-filled belly prevented the mangled steering wheel from fracturing her ribs and crushing her heart.

I first heard about Linda when her mother called to ask if the pregnancy center had any supplies to help them get started with baby care. She explained that they had not been prepared to bring a tiny baby home and needed some help to gather things. After she recovered and was home again, Linda came in a few times to talk and gather more resources. She moved back in with her parents, and after significant therapy, she was strong enough to work some hours again. Robert was the delight of his grandparents, who helped her care for him through the first years of his busy life. When I last saw Linda, she reported that Robert was doing well in school. He was already talking about becoming a first responder like his mom.

If you follow a certain line of popular thought, the world is full of "unwanted children." There are many poor children, undernourished children, and abused children. Some would argue that we should and can preselect the ones who should be born. The rest, those who might be born into difficult circumstances or with physical or mental limitations, are better off if they are eliminated before there is a chance that they will suffer any harm. If you follow any social media or watch tear-jerking TV shows about animals, you will find almost endless episodes about trapped beasts of all types who need rescuing. People are shown going to great trouble and some risk to get a pail off the head of a bear, or to cut a horned buck free of a wire fence, or to bring a frightened cat down from a high limb. Sometimes rescue squads arrive in expensive trucks and several people in protective gear gather to tackle the job. Police may arrive to stop traffic while a herd of elk cross the highway or to open a drain and rescue baby ducks who have fallen in and left their worried mother pacing on the edge of the pavement.

Somehow this attention always seems warranted and acceptable. It always tugs at our hearts. While hundreds of human babies are aborted every day, some people seem to be more concerned about maltreatment or distress in the animal kingdom and nonchalant about saving human babies. Why can't we care for all life and especially human life? One of the slogans that stirs my heart is, "Why can't we love them both?" This refers to loving both a mother and the child she is carrying. Shouldn't heroic action apply to the tiniest and most helpless of humans?

In the amazing Netflix documentary series *The Surgeon's Cut*, one of the four episodes tells the story of Dr. Kypros Nicolaides, a pioneer in fetal surgery.[10] Besides the incredible surgical methods used to save the lives of babies in utero, Nicolaides shows deep emotional involvement with his patients. He never grew weary of caring for them, of connecting

---

[10] *The Surgeon's Cut*. Season 1, "Saving Life Before Birth." Aired on Netflix September 9, 2020.

with them. He had a strong conviction about the importance of life. "A good surgeon," he says, "is one who knows how to approach the operation . . . one who knows how to think." He would think through all the possibilities for saving the life of each child, even if only one of a set of twins could be saved.

When you are tired and discouraged, and want to tell yourself another inspiring story, think about Dr. Nicolaides. Remember the importance of life, because you, too, are dealing with life and death. Approach each person with humble awe and empathetic sensitivity. Your intervention will not save every life, but it may bring someone closer to the God who alone can do that—for now and for eternity.

# CHAPTER 12

# Cultural Crisis

*We are on a roller-coaster ride.*

A forty-two-year-old medical doctor with a prestigious position at a city hospital came to our door unannounced. She did not want to give her name. She had seen our sign on her way to the train station and somewhat furtively stopped to see if we could help her in any way. She lived with her extended immigrant family, and she was one of the designated bread winners. The family was shaped by long-held patterns and traditions, and they had a strict code of honor. They had invested in her education and it was her duty now to help them all. There was no time in her life for romance or relationships or family of her own, and she knew she would never raise children. She wept as she shared her disappointment about that loss of opportunity.

Our client services director talked with her for more than thirty minutes. Then she came and asked me to join her to see if there was anything I could do for this client. The three of us spent another hour together.

The woman was sure she was pregnant, and her pregnancy test supported that. Wringing her hands in agony, she said she would have to have an abortion. Clearly wanting to keep the child, we talked with her through all the avenues of possible help. Her crying increased as she said, with bitter passion, "Nothing will help. They will kill me!" Nothing we could say calmed her as we tried to still her fears. We spoke of extreme measures, working through a system of Nurturing Network connections to find her a place to live and work in another part of the country with an assumed name and legal help to accomplish this. Terror gripped her, and she said they would find her wherever she went. They had ways and means, and she would surely be killed.

The father of this baby, who did not yet know she was pregnant, would go unpunished. He was a married family friend. They did not have a love affair; they just had sex. He would not, could not, protect her anyway. It did not matter to him, and he would say it was her responsibility to prevent the pregnancy or get rid of it. The family would not endure the shame of such an event, and there would be an honor killing. Honor was far more important than the generous income she earned. The shame was just too great.

We spoke to her of God's great love for her and of his ability to do things that seemed impossible. She accepted prayer and the assurance that we would be there to help her along the way, even ready to listen after an abortion if that is what she finally did. With clasped hands and bowed head, she thanked us profusely and said she would always think of us. She would not even take a card but knew she could always find us if needed.

The two of us sucked in silent sobs as she slipped out the door, checking nervously to see that no one was watching as she walked swiftly along the tall hedge and then stepped out to the sidewalk in front of the building next to us. *Her father really would kill her, and the mother who bore her would allow her to die needlessly.* There was not a thing that we could do. We had no name or address nor proof of coercion or crime. Just an overwhelming story about a sad and frightened woman who was going into the city to exercise her "free will" to choose abortion before anyone found out about her personal crisis. We continued to pray for her but never saw her again, though I carry a clear picture of her in my mind.

This was a stark and disturbing clash of cultural norms, something out of a textbook description that came alive right in front of us. It is hard for someone raised in our prevailing culture to think that such things can be allowed, even encouraged, and left unpunished in other parts of the world. It is startling to also see it settling into the neighborhood, hidden behind polite but distant smiles and formal greetings. It hints strongly at other things that are impacting the culture with which we are most familiar. I firmly believe that God has created each person and loves and cares for each one. Each people group and culture has value and contributes to the rich mosaic of life. I also believe that some things are patently wrong and violate the Creator's intent for mankind. Honor killing, genital mutilation, child sacrifice, and abortion are among them. Sadly, abortion is the one that is promoted within our own prevailing culture.

The culture all around us is in a state of vacillation. It has been happening over time and moving in subtle ways. Someone recently surprised me by saying that he had just gotten married this year and that he and his wife didn't have children yet because they had not lived together before they married. What an unusual comment that would have been fifty years ago! It would never have been openly assumed then that a couple might live together before the wedding. Now it is almost always expected.

There has been a sexual revolution, and restraints that were largely accepted half a century ago are no longer in place. Expectations have changed. Men who take a woman out for an evening and spend money on an event and a nice meal often feel entitled to sexual favors at the end. Women who are not clear inwardly about their own standards are more easily led to think they need to comply. Couples routinely move in together and try out their relationship. Why risk a binding commitment before they feel sure of each other? Since the biggest reason listed for getting a divorce is incompatibility, why not check that out first? Studies that track the rate of divorce after cohabitation before marriage are confusing in the conclusions they report. The variables of age and length of cohabitation and intent to marry or not all factor in, but we know that many cohabitation relationships do not last.

What I think is not factored in is the emotional impact of sexual intimacy and the possibility of pregnancy. Modern methods of birth control are not without failure rates, even when they are used consistently. With abortion lurking in the background as a way to "erase" an unplanned pregnancy, the risk of harm is exponentially greater. The woman who walked into our office that day was slated to pay an even higher price than usual because of how women were viewed in her culture.

Shame still lurks in any cultural context. We have not outgrown the concept or the intense pain that accompanies disappointed expectations, both our own and that of others. How sad that the conception of new life, one of the most powerful creative acts imaginable, continues to be fraught with deadly danger in all cultures.

# CHAPTER 13

# As Long as I Have Breath the Stories Continue

*There's always another opportunity and assignment.*

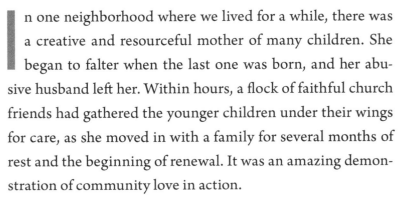

n one neighborhood where we lived for a while, there was a creative and resourceful mother of many children. She began to falter when the last one was born, and her abusive husband left her. Within hours, a flock of faithful church friends had gathered the younger children under their wings for care, as she moved in with a family for several months of rest and the beginning of renewal. It was an amazing demonstration of community love in action.

There was the unusual middle-aged newlywed couple who decided soon after marriage to have a baby, only to realize within a few months that the mother was not emotionally able to raise a child. They chose a brave adoption plan through a licensed adoption agency. The mother also asked for personal counsel through the pregnancy center.

There was the Spanish speaking woman who went into labor and needed to have an emergency C- section, but no one in the hospital could convince her to give consent. They even prevailed upon a dermatologist on duty who knew Spanish to try to explain it to her. Finally, she gave my name to a nurse who called me, and I went to the hospital. We had spent many hours together throughout her pregnancy and had managed to communicate. Now, in my broken Spanish, I had to convince her that the surgery was necessary to save the life of the baby because the umbilical cord was wrapped around his neck. I cajoled and prayed, and finally raised my voice and said, in Spanish, "Now is the time!" But my words were wrong, and I apparently said, "You are the time." That made her laugh, and she looked at me and said, "OK, *Jyouan*." The nurse rushed to have her sign the papers, and the doctor said, "Great! Your friend can go right into the operating room with us." It was the first surgery I ever witnessed, and I was deeply grateful and re- lieved that they provided a stool for me to sit on near her head where I could keep giving her reassurance and encouragement.

One young mother vacillated about parenting but finally chose adoption for her child. An adoption agency handled all the details, but she wanted her pregnancy advocate to come to see her in the hospital. We had a tender time as she held her little girl and then relinquished her to the nurses and prepared to leave. She left with her mother, but her stepfather lingered long enough to dump a load of harsh words on me for "allowing" her to see and hold the infant. I remember crying all the way home in the heavy traffic of a Friday afternoon. His words could be ignored, but her tears tugged at my heart.

Our center was well established with three suburban locations. It became a personal mission to work with Care Net to help establish a new center deep inside the city where the need was great. That called for trips downtown for organizational meetings and training seminars and work on another board of directors. The work was challenging and exhilarating. The surrounding population was vulnerable to the easy accessibility and strong pressure to abort unplanned pregnancies. There was an eager cadre of women and men who wanted to provide education and help to encourage the choice for life. With committed leadership from the top down, there was energy and determination to provide a place within the community that would offer a better alternative. We were able to celebrate the grand opening of that center, which was located just blocks away from an infamous and filthy abortion clinic which has since been closed.

There are the stories *you* could tell that multiply these illustrations by the hundreds of thousands and could fill many books—stories that will breed hope and bring life to countless others. People need to know what you are doing to make changes for the better in this troubled world. Write your stories and share them. Let your testimonies stir the hearts of others and motivate their active care for young and old, the born and unborn. Be doers of the Word of God.

## Missed Opportunities

As I look back over the years, stories surface and rumble through my mind. Although I am primarily grateful for the varied and rich experiences I have had, I am keenly aware of opportunities that were missed. There were people I ignored and did not encourage, times when I grew weary and turned aside events that offered creative opportunities that I did not seize. The following simple story is one that I have often smiled about but can look back and see some missed creative opportunities.

The children were settling into their bunk beds and ready for their nightly story. These four cousins were having a wild summer together, playing outdoors and ranging through the woods. They rarely had enough time together since they were usually separated by half a continent, but now they had weeks to play endlessly while two of the cousins' parents were on an extensive trip.

On this particular evening, I was about halfway through reading them a story when I felt something moving at my side. I was wearing a long, silky robe, and I reached down to see what was going on as I continued to read. There was something there, right at my side now. I captured it in my hand through the slippery material so I could check it out when I was done.

After all, the story had to be finished, and we were right near the climax.

We were living in a rural communal setting that served the needs of a number of people. The bunk room we were in was located in the main building, which was an old, repurposed barn. There were some older students up on the third floor, and our bedroom was just down the hall from the bunk room. I finished the exciting tale and gave each child a hug, certain that it would be a while before they stopped giggling and really settled in for the night, even though they were tired from their adventures.

I slipped into the bathroom to lift up my robe and find out what was inside my little bundle. There lay a tiny hairless naked baby mouse, and I showed it to the laughing children. The little creature was so defenseless and cute. Now I had to figure out what to do. We were always waging a war with the mice, setting traps in the storage area and in the closets in the kitchen. I could never get this itty bitty one back to its original nest, and then I would wonder anyway which trap would eventually get it in the end. So I flushed it down the toilet!

The story was fun to tell, and there were lots of comments about how calm I stayed and how I could possibly have kept on reading. As I muse about it after so many years, I realize what an opportunity I had missed. Although the children were seeing and petting and feeding all kinds of animals every day, this could have been their first pet mouse. I can imagine them making a little cage for it, finding food to feed it, and nursing it into adulthood. We could have done some study on the life and times of a country mouse and held a contest to name it. We did some plays and programs that summer, which entertained the adults greatly. Little mouse could certainly have had a starring role in one of them.

As simple as it seems, this silly tale makes me wonder about all the other missed opportunities I have had in my life. There are always lessons to learn and different ways to see situations. There is so much more of life to be discovered, and we miss much of it. I, for one, have often held back with fear and un-certainty, shutting things down without enough curiosity and exploration. I want to tidy things up and put them in order, as long as I have one space to make messes in on my own. This pattern goes way back for me, and my father saw it when I was a child. I was afraid of new things, he said. I still am, really, even though other people comment about how much change and adventure I have actually experienced.

Helping other people is an adventure in itself. Each new contact brings all kinds of unknown possibilities. Some are dangerous and sad. Some are tremendously fulfilling and re-warding. All need to be passed through the light of God's love and care and received with his blessing.

I am just one of a huge congregation of people who have a call to help other people. I know many who come alongside others in tremendously practical ways. Those who build and dig and mow and cook and clean and give tender nursing care are inspirational. Those who teach and mentor and study and design provide an awesome amount of help to others. Those who listen and empathize and pray help to round out the picture.

As I have been writing this book, I have found restless times in the night to be very productive. I write in my mind and wake later to write it down. One night I woke with a vivid and disturbing dream. I was at some large event and had excused myself to go to the ladies' room. As I approached the door, it was suddenly flung open, and a disheveled and tearful woman pushed past me and ran down the hall. When I entered, I saw a pool of blood on the floor in a stall and heard a faint cry. There on the cold tile floor was a newborn baby, struggling for life with the placenta still attached. I took off my long wool scarf and wrapped the child up quickly, trying frantically to wipe off her face and keep the airway clear. Someone else entered and called 911 immediately. Help came in time to provide the care that saved the baby's life. The distraught mother was identified and treated also.

Much of our helping is like that. We may be the first on the scene, but others are needed to carry on after us. Conclusions matter, but we do not get to read them all to know the outcomes. We step on the moving train and get off at some specified destination, while others ride on and new people enter. What matters is that we get on in the first place. We are not responsible for the end of the story, but we need to get into the action when the door of the opportunity opens.

Those who want to serve God are called to do so with

honesty and humility. I wrote the following article, which was published in the winter of 2007 in Care Net's *Center of Tomorrow* journal.[11] I've been given permission by Care Net to use it again. I'm sharing it with you as a personal learning experience that profoundly deepened my understanding of and commitment to authentic servanthood.

## The Green Corduroy Coat

We know little of servanthood. Something is entirely missing from our present experience, as well as from the romanticized world of novels where servants moved within their own society "in service" in an under-culture with its own rigid patterns and rules. Images of Downton Abbey come to my mind. Servanthood in the biblical sense is an entirely different thing. The Christian is called to serve the living God but is most adept at serving only the god of self. Serving God is not a part-time affair. There is no other "real" life for the off-duty hours.

The valued servant is always vigilant, looking for the slightest indicators to ascertain the wishes of the one served. At the heart of the matter is a deep desire to please, to anticipate, to respond without hesitation. There are no unacceptable tasks or restricted areas. This is not a stepping-stone to a different goal, though advancement is the promotion from true servant to friend. Jesus puts it this way to his inner circle of companions:

---

[11] Boydell, Joan E. "The Green Corduroy Coat." Care Net *Center of Tomorrow* III, No. 1 (2007).

*I no longer call you servants, because a servant does not know his master's business. Instead, I have called you friends, for everything that I have learned from my Father I have made known to you.*

— John 15:15 (NIV)

A few years after I started as executive director of the pregnancy center, we relocated to a new building. Finally, we had excellent basement space to store material goods for our clients. When most of the other rooms were in some semblance of order, the basement was still a disaster area. Coinciding with the move was a huge influx of random donations. We were suddenly "blessed" with bags full of clothing we do not stock for distribution, such as non-maternity items and outfits for older children. It still had to be sorted and hauled away to the thrift shop.

Near the end of a hectic Friday afternoon, a woman called because she needed shoes and diapers for her one-year-old. She had great difficulty understanding our directions, but she was borrowing a car and hoped to be there by 4:30. We doubted she would make it, but we prepared to see her. At 4:15, a walk-in client arrived. I was deep into a pile of important matters I was determined to complete before the weekend. Not wishing to be distracted, I suggested our counselor take the walk-in, and I would quickly help the other woman—if she found us.

At 4:45 she was at the door. There were four other children

with her besides the infant. They were unruly and unkempt. Because she was unable to read, all the intake information had to be carefully read and explained.

I was still struggling with my own attitude problem regarding my important work when I suggested we all go downstairs. The disordered mess was oppressive to me, and all the children began to tear into the boxes and rummage through the profusion of goods.

We did find shoes for the baby, but there were no diapers. I began at last to really pray and ask God to help me. The four-year-old found a pretty dress and eyed it with wonder. My heart softened quickly as she asked wistfully if she could have it. Finally engaged, I plowed into the piles in earnest. Because we had so much, we were able to find something for everyone. There were even slippers and a nightgown for the twelve-year-old and a robe for the mother.

We were talking and laughing together as we finished bagging the transformed treasures and prepared to pack the car. Suddenly the mother eyed the maternity clothes and took a coat off the rack. This was no ordinary coat. It was a beautifully styled green corduroy cape coat that some wealthy woman had worn in the later stages of pregnancy. I had admired it when it came in and pictured giving it to some pretty young pregnant woman to wear this winter.

"Can I have this?" said the disheveled woman.

I felt my heart scrunch right down inside of me. Hesitating,

I said, "That coat was given so someone who was pregnant could wear it throughout her pregnancy."

"But anyone can wear this kind," she eagerly replied, "And I ain't got no coat." I had a fleeting glimpse of this tattered woman arrayed absurdly in such a fine coat, and then I saw the sparkle of delight in her eyes. I packed it with the rest of the things and sent her on the way, soon forgetting the whole encounter.

A week later, I sat with some friends as we studied and discussed the book of James. Someone finished reading James 1:27 about God's pleasure when we care for widows and orphans, and I started reading Chapter 2.

> *My brothers and sisters, believers in our glorious Lord Jesus Christ must not show favoritism. Suppose a man comes into your meeting wearing a gold ring and fine clothes, and a poor man in filthy old clothes also comes in. If you show special attention to the man wearing fine clothes and say, "Here's a good seat for you," but say to the poor man, "You stand there" or "Sit on the floor by my feet," have you not discriminated among yourselves and become judges with evil thoughts?*
>
> — James 2:1–4 (NIV)

I began to think about that green corduroy coat. The Lord delivered a gentle but challenging message to me over the next few days. It was clear as could be: "Joan, my daughter, I left my throne in heaven and cast aside my royal robes to come to earth and sacrifice myself for you. I have thrown my cloak of love and protection over you. Now what is it in you that made you hesitate to give a desperately needy woman a green corduroy coat?"

The woman had been right in saying "anyone could wear that coat." The awful answer to God's question was that it had crossed my mind that if someone did not pick out that coat soon, maybe I should try it on myself. Imagine that!

How grateful I am that God has not given up on me. How grateful I am that his training ground for servanthood is still active in my life so that He may someday more perfectly form in me the true heart of a servant.

As we consider all the events of life and the service we have often given so feebly, we can also look to what lies ahead. As I bring this book of stories to a close, I share one last story to you as encouragement and blessing to you for what lies ahead. It is part of my own story of growing in the relentless pursuit of my heart and mind by One who loves me more than I can imagine.

## Jewels in the Closet

When we did not hear from some dear friends at Christmas and several phone calls went unanswered, we called our friends' son to find out about them. Our male friend had recently died, and his wife was now in the memory care unit at the care facility they had moved to, unresponsive now to her own children and grandchildren.

As I mused over the sad loss of this deep and long-term temporal friendship, I remembered a dream I had on one of our visits to their home.

It was a vivid dream. I was sleeping soundly in my friend's guest room when I dreamed I got out of bed and quietly opened the closet door. There I was amazed to see a brilliant display of magnificent jewels. They were piled high on the shelves and spilling onto the floor in waves. Some were strung and draped over hangers or filling baskets, the brilliant colors glimmering in the faint light from the streetlamp seeping in around the window shades. The sheer abundance overwhelmed me. I had looked in this closet before, and nothing like this was evident. Who had put them there? Why hadn't I seen any before?

My first thought was to awaken my husband, so he could enjoy this splendor, but the dream was quickly fading, and I drifted back to sleep. At full light I awoke, and the memory of the dream was fresh. I hesitated to open the closet, knowing that I would no longer see the treasure. *Or would I?* I wondered. Wasn't the treasure really there all around me? I had been missing it, rushing through life and work and concerns, while the precious gems glinted in the corners while I raced by. It was time, I knew, to look again.

We were spending two nights with these friends in Georgia, on our way to Florida and then planning to return home by driving along the coast. We had become friends during navy days, early in our marriages. For two years, both men were stationed at Pearl Harbor. They would leave on three-month rotations as part of a crew on a nuclear submarine that docked in Guam. Our husbands shared a compact closet for their living space, while we wives occupied comfortable homes overlooking the volcanic mountains and Pacific Ocean on the northeast side of Oahu. She had two small children, and I was expecting my first. We spent many nights in each other's homes, and on impromptu visits, her little ones wore my husband's undershirts for pajamas. Over the years we settled in different parts of the country and had much less contact, but those early days of friendship were important stepping-stones in our lives.

More than fifty years had passed. We went to share some time in a Saratoga beach house with these dear friends to help celebrate their fiftieth anniversary a few years ago. The next year we invited them to share a week with us at a timeshare. Now we were making a number of nostalgic trips to visit friends who were important to us during our fifty years of marriage. On the Saratoga visit we were told that she had a mild cognitive decline. By the time-share visit a year later, the decline was more evident, and we shared tears and sad laughter over the ways this was affecting her and their life together. Now in her guest room, with my heart aching for the beautiful person I was watching going through this unwanted struggle, I find this treasure trove.

I heard the Lord whisper, "Look at it, Joan. Look at the

wealth of beauty, wisdom, and joy piled up here. Look at the intricate design of each precious piece. See it displayed in its proper glory, ready to adorn kings and queens in regal attire. Do you know what you have? Do you even have the slightest notion of what it means to revel in being part of my family? Have you given consideration to the enormous wealth of your family of believers? It is time to look more closely at the jewels strewn at your feet, surrounding you in abundance, enriching your life beyond measure."

These friends had given years of their lives to reach out to others in countries around the world with the message of love and forgiveness of the Gospel of Jesus Christ. Of course, there are jewels in their closet, gathered over the years and stored in the treasure house of God for eternity. Did you know that you, people helpers and servants of God, have a treasure trove also? It is waiting to be revealed when you finally arrive at the feet of Jesus.

*Little children, little children,*
*Who love their Redeemer,*
*Are the jewels, precious jewels,*
*His loved and His own.*
*Like the stars of the morning,*
*His bright crown adorning,*
*They will shine in his beauty.*
*Bright gems for his crown.*

— William O. Cushing, 1856

Perhaps the words of an ancient and yet profoundly contemporary prophet, spoken more than 2700 years ago, capture more eloquently and powerfully than Cushing's song, words of truth and hope so needed in our times:

> *Can a mother forget her baby at her breast and have no compassion on the child she has borne? Though she may forget, I will not forget you. See, I have engraved you on the palms of my hands; your walls are ever before me.*

> *The children born during your bereavement will yet say in your hearing: "This place is too small for us; give us more space to live in." Then you will say in your heart, "Who bore me these? I was bereaved and barren; I was exiled and rejected. Who brought these up? I was left all alone, but these—where have they come from?"*

> *This is what the Sovereign Lord says: "See, I will beckon to the Gentiles; I will lift up my banner to the peoples; they will bring your sons in their arms and carry your daughters on their shoulders. Kings will be your foster fathers, and their queens your nursing mothers. They will bow down before you with their faces to the ground; they will lick the dust at your feet. Then you will know that I*

*am the Lord, those who hope in me will not be disappointed."*

— Isaiah 49:15–16, 20–23 (NIV)

*This I know. It is true for me, and for you, too!*

*My Father will not kill me!*
He is not ashamed of me, and he calls me to his side.
His love is everlasting, and He delights in me!

*My Mother will not die!*
The one who birthed me and nourishes me will
never abandon me but refreshes me daily!

# About the Author

J oan Boydell enjoyed a childhood in a hardworking, lower-middle-class family full of love and parental encouragement. Drawn toward higher education, she earned her BA degree in English literature at Wheaton College, where she grew not only intellectually, socially, and spiritually, but gained confidence in serving the needs of others. Prompted to serve beyond her college community, Joan spent the summer between her junior and senior years in an internship with Wycliff Bible Translators in Guatemala, where she improved her competence in Spanish and gained some understanding of the environment of developing countries and communities and the value of teamwork.

She continued her studies with graduate level education at Immaculata University, earning an MA degree in counseling psychology and meeting the licensing requirements to become a licensed professional counselor. At the same time, Joan was hired into the role of executive director at a nearby pregnancy center, in which she served almost twenty years, helping men and women facing unplanned pregnancy situations under-stand the value of making life-giving decisions.

Under her leadership, the center saw the addition of satellite centers in the region, the expansion of its offerings to include post-abortion ministry, the building of a high-performance staff and an enthusiastic team of volunteers, and a reputation for integrity and service within the region. Based on her exten-sive experience training counselors and teaching workshops she was offered and accepted the opportunity to be a con-tracted consultant for Care Net, an oversight and resource organization with more than 1000 affiliated centers. She has served in that capacity for twenty-seven years, bringing her wisdom and knowledge to their boards, executive directors, staff, and volunteers.

She now provides local private counseling on a limited ba-sis through her business, Joan Boydell, Licensed Professional Counseling, where she can continue the important work of en-couraging and equipping individuals toward a wisdom-filled life.

She and her husband of fifty-six years, Bruce Boydell, con-tinue to be involved in their local church and enjoy the fellow-ship of faithful and caring friends and family. While living a busy and productive life and experiencing the fruit of diligent preparation and previous experiences, Joan is continuing to grow in her love of God and her precious family, which now includes three granddaughters.

To God belongs the glory and the credit for whatever way

her book might benefit you. Through the redemptive passion, death, and resurrection of Jesus Christ, come the hope and confidence that lives marked by trauma, pain, rejection, and failure can be restored and become a harvest that reflects the unfailing and relentless pursue of LOVE.

If you would like to contact Joan to ask questions or to start a conversation, you may email her at jeboydellbook@ gmail.com.

# Many Thanks Due

hank you to the people who took the time to read this book and write endorsements that I hope will encourage many others to read it.

A circle of dear friends from different places and situations over the years encouraged me to write this book and gladly read the early manuscripts. Their comments, questions, upgrades, and prayers helped the book take shape. Thank you!

Dottie Wobb and Sue Fultz have both been consultants and trainers for Care Net. They also served as executive directors of pregnancy centers and we have communicated well over the years. They have both also been great roommates at Care Net Conferences, where we learn and laugh together! These ladies have both been highly involved in women's ministry for many years. Sue is also the author of a recent book, *Leading for Life*.

Jane "Goldie" Winn was a close colleague during my years as Executive Director of a pregnancy center. She shared in some of the stories contained in this book.

I also want to thank Meredith Bowman, friend and former

work colleague, for directing us to Beth Lottig who added her professional expertise and passion to the final editing stages.

As I moved to different places, we bonded with new friends in small groups at the churches we attended. Margene Sorzano, a reading specialist, has a gift of hospitality and opens her home to welcome in study groups. She continues to keep a large group of mutual friends well connected.

Marliss Berke, a high school counselor, and Heidi Eisenhard, a Grief Share and caregiving leader, became dear friends when we lived in the mountains. We are enjoying growing older together, sharing good books and great memories.

Last but surely not least, my daughter and close friend, Amy Boydell Zorrilla, is a constant source of joy and wisdom in my life. Her daughter Beatrice, our first grandchild, contributed her artwork and design gifts to the cover!

# Recommended Reading

Boydell, Bruce J. *Right Full Rudder: Courage to Change Course.* Lifespan Coaching & Consulting, LLC, 2017.

Bergner, Daniel. *Sing For Your Life: A story of Race, Music, and Family.* New York: Little Brown & Company, 2016.

Collins, R. Dandridge, PhD. *The Trauma Zone: Trusting God For Emotional Healing.* Chicago: Moody Publishers, January 2009.

Gabodo-Madikizela, Pumla. *A South African Woman Confronts the Legacy of Apartheid.* New York: Houghton Mifflin, 2003

Goulston, Mark. *Just Listen: Discover the Secret to Getting Through to Absolutely Anyone.* New York: Amacom, 2010.

Harris, Nadine Burke, MD. *The Deepest Well: Healing the Long-Term Effects of Childhood Adversity.* Boston: Marine Books, 2019, New York: Houghton Mifflin Harcourt, 2018.

Perry, Bruce D., MD PhD, and Szalavitz, Maria. *The Boy Who Was Raised As A Dog: and Other Stories from a Psychiatrist's Notebook*. New York: Basic Books, 2017.

Strong, Marilee. *A Bright Red Scream: Self-Mutilation and the Language of Pain*. New York: Penguin Group, 1999.

CPSIA information can be obtained
at www.ICGtesting.com
Printed in the USA
BVHW061531040222
627690BV00006B/12